TEACHER'S PET PUBLICATIONS

PUZZLE PACK
for
Maniac Magee

based on the book by
Jerry Spinelli

Written by
William T. Collins

© 2005 Teacher's Pet Publications
All Rights Reserved

The materials in this packet are copyrighted
by Teacher's Pet Publications, Inc.

These pages may be duplicated by the purchaser
for use in the purchaser's own classroom.

Copying any of these materials and distributing them
for any other purpose is a violation of the copyright laws.

© 2005 Teacher's Pet Publications, Inc.
www.tpet.com

INTRODUCTION
If you already own the LitPlan for this title, this Puzzle Pack will refresh your Unit Resource Materials and Vocabulary Resource Materials sections plus give you additional materials you can substitute into the tests. If you do not already have a complete LitPlan, these pages will give you some supplemental materials to use with your own plan. There are two main groups of materials: one set for unit words (such as characters' names, symbols, places, etc.) and one set for vocabulary words associated with the book.

WORD LIST
There is a word list for both the unit words and the vocabulary words. These lists show you which words are being used in the materials and the clues or definitions being used for those words. You may want to give students a word list with clues/definitions to help them, or you may want students to only have a word list (without clues/definitions) if you want them to work a little harder. Both are available for duplication. The word lists can also be your "calling key" for the bingo games.

FILL IN THE BLANK AND MATCHING
There are 4 each of the fill in the blank and matching worksheets for both the unit and vocabulary words. These pages can be used either as extra worksheets for students or as objective parts of a unit test. They can be done individually if students need extra help or as a whole class activity to review the material covered.

MAGIC SQUARES
The magic squares not only reinforce the material covered but also work on reasoning and math skills. Many teachers have told us that their students really enjoy doing these!

WORD SEARCH PUZZLES
The word search words go in all directions, as indicated on your answer keys. Two of the word search puzzles have the clues listed rather than the words. This makes the puzzle a little more difficult, but it reinforces the material better. Two word search puzzles have words only for students who find the clue puzzles too difficult.

CROSSWORD PUZZLES
Both unit and vocabulary word sections have 4 crossword puzzles.

BINGO CARDS
There are 32 individual bingo cards for the unit words and 32 individual bingo cards for the vocabulary words. You can use your word list as a "call list," calling the words at random and marking them off of your list as you go, or you could use the flash cards by cutting them apart and drawing the words at random from a hat (or box or whatever). To make a better review, you might ask for the definition and spelling of each word as you call it out–or you could call out the definitions and have students tell you the words they need to look for on the puzzle.

JUGGLE LETTERS
The vocabulary juggle letter game is intended to help students learn the spellings of the words. One sheet has the definitions listed on it as an extra help for students who need it or to reinforce the definitions if you choose to do so.

FLASH CARDS
We've included a set of vocabulary flash cards you can duplicate, cut, and fold for your students. Some teachers make a few sets for general use by the class; others make a set for each student. Some teachers duplicate them for each student and have the students cut & fold their own. You can cut out just the words and put them in a hat, have each student pick out one word and write the definition and a sentence for that word. Students then swap words and papers, with the next student adding a sentence of his own under the last one. You can have students swap as many times as you like. Each time the student will read the sentences written prior to his own and then add a sentence. You can cut out the words and definitions separately and play "I Have; Who Has?" Each student in the room draws a word and definition. The first student says, "I have (the name of the word). Who has the definition?" The student with the definition reads it then says, "I have (the name of the vocabulary word she has). Who has the definition?" The round continues until all words and definitions have been given.

Maniac Magee Unit Word List

No.	Word	Clue/Definition
1.	AMANDA	She had a suitcase full of books
2.	ARNOLD	High school kids put him in Finsterwald's yard
3.	BAND	Maniac lived there when he knew Grayson: ___ shell
4.	BATH	Maniac took one every night with Hester and Lester
5.	BETHANY	Church where Manic went with the Beales
6.	BRIAN	Star quarterback
7.	BRIDGEPORT	Where Jeffrey was born
8.	BUFFALO	Maniac kissed a baby one
9.	COBRAS	McNab's group of friends
10.	CONFETTI	Someone used Amanda's book to make it
11.	CONSONANTS	Easy for Grayson to learn
12.	CONTENT	How Maniac felt at the end of the story
13.	COULD	First book Grayson read: The Little Engine That ___
14.	CRUSADE	Title of book Maniac borrowed from Amanda: Children's ___
15.	DAN	Uncle ___ didn't talk to his wife
16.	DOT	Aunt ___ hated her husband
17.	DUMP	Maniac walked barefoot through it
18.	EAST	End where the blacks lived
19.	ELMWOOD	Where Maniac slept at first: ___ Park Zoo
20.	ENCYCLOPEDIA	Maniac got up early to read it
21.	FINSTERWALD	Scary house in East End
22.	FROGBALL	Maniac logged the world's first one
23.	GEORGE	Called Mars Bar IT
24.	GLOVE	Grayson's Christmas present to Maniac
25.	GRAYSON	Taught Maniac to play baseball
26.	HANDS	Receiver doing a fly pattern: ___ down
27.	HECTOR	Street that divided the East and West Ends
28.	HESTER	Amanda's 4 year old sister
29.	HOLLIDAYSBURG	Where Maniac's aunt and uncle lived
30.	HYDRANT	Kids had a swimming party there: fire ___
31.	JEFFREY	Maniac's real first name
32.	JOHN	Largest player in the Little League
33.	KNOT	Made of string with lots of contortions: cobble's ___
34.	KRIMPETS	Maniac liked to eat butterscotch ones
35.	LESTER	Amanda's 3 year old brother
36.	LIBRARY	Amanda said Maniac could not get this card without an address
37.	LIONEL	Jeffrey's middle name
38.	MARS	Went to the McNab house with Maniac: ___ Bar
39.	MAYS	The book Maniac wrote for Grayson: The Man Who Struck Out Willie ___
40.	MILLS	Where Jeffrey ended up: Two ___
41.	MINORS	Where Grayson played baseball
42.	MIRACLE	Jeffrey kept his room clean
43.	MULLIGAN	Grayson's favorite book: Mike ___ and His Steam Shovel
44.	NAME	Jeffrey was afraid of losing it
45.	PICKWELLS	Maniac and Mars Bar ate dinner with them
46.	PILLBOX	McNabs were building one in their living room
47.	PIPER	Invited Maniac to his birthday party
48.	PITCHER	Grayson's position
49.	PIZZA	Maniac was allergic to it
50.	POLKAS	Music Maniac and Grayson listened to
51.	PROTECTORS	Maniac slept on them: chest ___
52.	RAN	Jeffrey did this early in the morning, all over town

Maniac Magee Unit Word List

No.	Word	Clue/Definition
53.	READ	Maniac taught Grayson to do it
54.	RUSSELL	Stuck on the trolley trestle
55.	SCHUYLKILL	The trolley car fell off the track and into this river
56.	SCREAM	Jeffrey did it during the concert
57.	SNICKERS	Amanda said she was changing Mars Bar's name to this
58.	SYCAMORE	The Beale family lived on this street
59.	THOMPSON	Mars Bar's last name
60.	THREE	Age when Jeffrey became an orphan
61.	TRAIN	Maniac raced it and won
62.	TRASH	Mrs. Beale didn't want Maniac using this kind of talk in her house
63.	TRESTLE	Russell was stuck on it
64.	VALLEY	Maniac went to ___ Forge to wait for death
65.	VOWELS	These were hard for Grayson to learn
66.	YMCA	Grayson lived there when he met Maniac

Maniac Magee Fill In The Blank 1

_____ 1. Kids had a swimming party there: fire ___

_____ 2. Grayson's favorite book: Mike ___ and His Steam Shovel

_____ 3. Maniac taught Grayson to do it

_____ 4. Maniac's real first name

_____ 5. Maniac got up early to read it

_____ 6. The book Maniac wrote for Grayson: The Man Who Struck Out Willie ___

_____ 7. Where Grayson played baseball

_____ 8. Mars Bar's last name

_____ 9. She had a suitcase full of books

_____ 10. Scary house in East End

_____ 11. Where Jeffrey was born

_____ 12. Music Maniac and Grayson listened to

_____ 13. The Beale family lived on this street

_____ 14. High school kids put him in Finsterwald's yard

_____ 15. Amanda's 3 year old brother

_____ 16. These were hard for Grayson to learn

_____ 17. Street that divided the East and West Ends

_____ 18. Grayson's position

_____ 19. Maniac raced it and won

_____ 20. Church where Manic went with the Beales

Maniac Magee Fill In The Blank 1 Answer Key

HYDRANT	1. Kids had a swimming party there: fire ___
MULLIGAN	2. Grayson's favorite book: Mike ___ and His Steam Shovel
READ	3. Maniac taught Grayson to do it
JEFFREY	4. Maniac's real first name
ENCYCLOPEDIA	5. Maniac got up early to read it
MAYS	6. The book Maniac wrote for Grayson: The Man Who Struck Out Willie ___
MINORS	7. Where Grayson played baseball
THOMPSON	8. Mars Bar's last name
AMANDA	9. She had a suitcase full of books
FINSTERWALD	10. Scary house in East End
BRIDGEPORT	11. Where Jeffrey was born
POLKAS	12. Music Maniac and Grayson listened to
SYCAMORE	13. The Beale family lived on this street
ARNOLD	14. High school kids put him in Finsterwald's yard
LESTER	15. Amanda's 3 year old brother
VOWELS	16. These were hard for Grayson to learn
HECTOR	17. Street that divided the East and West Ends
PITCHER	18. Grayson's position
TRAIN	19. Maniac raced it and won
BETHANY	20. Church where Manic went with the Beales

Maniac Magee Fill In The Blank 2

1. McNab's group of friends
2. Maniac liked to eat butterscotch ones
3. Where Jeffrey was born
4. Largest player in the Little League
5. Jeffrey was afraid of losing it
6. Easy for Grayson to learn
7. Grayson's Christmas present to Maniac
8. Church where Manic went with the Beales
9. Maniac raced it and won
10. Jeffrey's middle name
11. Maniac walked barefoot through it
12. The Beale family lived on this street
13. Someone used Amanda's book to make it
14. Maniac went to ___ Forge to wait for death
15. Maniac's real first name
16. The trolley car fell off the track and into this river
17. Maniac was allergic to it
18. Maniac took one every night with Hester and Lester
19. Title of book Maniac borrowed from Amanda: Children's ___
20. Street that divided the East and West Ends

Maniac Magee Fill In The Blank 2 Answer Key

COBRAS	1. McNab's group of friends
KRIMPETS	2. Maniac liked to eat butterscotch ones
BRIDGEPORT	3. Where Jeffrey was born
JOHN	4. Largest player in the Little League
NAME	5. Jeffrey was afraid of losing it
CONSONANTS	6. Easy for Grayson to learn
GLOVE	7. Grayson's Christmas present to Maniac
BETHANY	8. Church where Manic went with the Beales
TRAIN	9. Maniac raced it and won
LIONEL	10. Jeffrey's middle name
DUMP	11. Maniac walked barefoot through it
SYCAMORE	12. The Beale family lived on this street
CONFETTI	13. Someone used Amanda's book to make it
VALLEY	14. Maniac went to ___ Forge to wait for death
JEFFREY	15. Maniac's real first name
SCHUYLKILL	16. The trolley car fell off the track and into this river
PIZZA	17. Maniac was allergic to it
BATH	18. Maniac took one every night with Hester and Lester
CRUSADE	19. Title of book Maniac borrowed from Amanda: Children's ___
HECTOR	20. Street that divided the East and West Ends

Maniac Magee Fill In The Blank 3

_____ 1. Title of book Maniac borrowed from Amanda: Children's ___

_____ 2. Receiver doing a fly pattern: ___ down

_____ 3. Taught Maniac to play baseball

_____ 4. McNab's group of friends

_____ 5. Music Maniac and Grayson listened to

_____ 6. Amanda said Maniac could not get this card without an address

_____ 7. Made of string with lots of contortions: cobble's ___

_____ 8. Maniac taught Grayson to do it

_____ 9. The book Maniac wrote for Grayson: The Man Who Struck Out Willie ___

_____ 10. Jeffrey was afraid of losing it

_____ 11. Maniac raced it and won

_____ 12. Where Jeffrey was born

_____ 13. Maniac kissed a baby one

_____ 14. Age when Jeffrey became an orphan

_____ 15. Amanda said she was changing Mars Bar's name to this

_____ 16. Maniac and Mars Bar ate dinner with them

_____ 17. Maniac took one every night with Hester and Lester

_____ 18. Jeffrey's middle name

_____ 19. Mars Bar's last name

_____ 20. Maniac walked barefoot through it

Maniac Magee Fill In The Blank 3 Answer Key

CRUSADE	1. Title of book Maniac borrowed from Amanda: Children's ___
HANDS	2. Receiver doing a fly pattern: ___ down
GRAYSON	3. Taught Maniac to play baseball
COBRAS	4. McNab's group of friends
POLKAS	5. Music Maniac and Grayson listened to
LIBRARY	6. Amanda said Maniac could not get this card without an address
KNOT	7. Made of string with lots of contortions: cobble's ___
READ	8. Maniac taught Grayson to do it
MAYS	9. The book Maniac wrote for Grayson: The Man Who Struck Out Willie ___
NAME	10. Jeffrey was afraid of losing it
TRAIN	11. Maniac raced it and won
BRIDGEPORT	12. Where Jeffrey was born
BUFFALO	13. Maniac kissed a baby one
THREE	14. Age when Jeffrey became an orphan
SNICKERS	15. Amanda said she was changing Mars Bar's name to this
PICKWELLS	16. Maniac and Mars Bar ate dinner with them
BATH	17. Maniac took one every night with Hester and Lester
LIONEL	18. Jeffrey's middle name
THOMPSON	19. Mars Bar's last name
DUMP	20. Maniac walked barefoot through it

Maniac Magee Fill In The Blank 4

_____   1. Aunt ___ hated her husband

_____   2. Made of string with lots of contortions: cobble's ___

_____   3. Kids had a swimming party there: fire ___

_____   4. She had a suitcase full of books

_____   5. Mrs. Beale didn't want Maniac using this kind of talk in her house

_____   6. Amanda's 4 year old sister

_____   7. Where Jeffrey ended up: Two ___

_____   8. Grayson lived there when he met Maniac

_____   9. Title of book Maniac borrowed from Amanda: Children's ___

_____   10. Jeffrey's middle name

_____   11. The Beale family lived on this street

_____   12. Where Grayson played baseball

_____   13. Went to the McNab house with Maniac: ___ Bar

_____   14. Age when Jeffrey became an orphan

_____   15. Maniac got up early to read it

_____   16. Street that divided the East and West Ends

_____   17. Taught Maniac to play baseball

_____   18. Russell was stuck on it

_____   19. Jeffrey did it during the concert

_____   20. Church where Manic went with the Beales

Maniac Magee Fill In The Blank 4 Answer Key

DOT	1. Aunt ___ hated her husband
KNOT	2. Made of string with lots of contortions: cobble's ___
HYDRANT	3. Kids had a swimming party there: fire ___
AMANDA	4. She had a suitcase full of books
TRASH	5. Mrs. Beale didn't want Maniac using this kind of talk in her house
HESTER	6. Amanda's 4 year old sister
MILLS	7. Where Jeffrey ended up: Two ___
YMCA	8. Grayson lived there when he met Maniac
CRUSADE	9. Title of book Maniac borrowed from Amanda: Children's ___
LIONEL	10. Jeffrey's middle name
SYCAMORE	11. The Beale family lived on this street
MINORS	12. Where Grayson played baseball
MARS	13. Went to the McNab house with Maniac: ___ Bar
THREE	14. Age when Jeffrey became an orphan
ENCYCLOPEDIA	15. Maniac got up early to read it
HECTOR	16. Street that divided the East and West Ends
GRAYSON	17. Taught Maniac to play baseball
TRESTLE	18. Russell was stuck on it
SCREAM	19. Jeffrey did it during the concert
BETHANY	20. Church where Manic went with the Beales

Maniac Magee Matching 1

___ 1. THOMPSON   A. Taught Maniac to play baseball
___ 2. GRAYSON   B. Star quarterback
___ 3. NAME   C. Jeffrey kept his room clean
___ 4. FINSTERWALD   D. Jeffrey's middle name
___ 5. PIPER   E. These were hard for Grayson to learn
___ 6. PROTECTORS   F. McNabs were building one in their living room
___ 7. RAN   G. Age when Jeffrey became an orphan
___ 8. MINORS   H. Music Maniac and Grayson listened to
___ 9. CONTENT   I. Someone used Amanda's book to make it
___10. CONFETTI   J. Kids had a swimming party there: fire ___
___11. RUSSELL   K. Scary house in East End
___12. MIRACLE   L. Mars Bar's last name
___13. VALLEY   M. Where Grayson played baseball
___14. LIONEL   N. Stuck on the trolley trestle
___15. BRIAN   O. Maniac slept on them: chest ___
___16. MAYS   P. Maniac went to ___ Forge to wait for death
___17. BRIDGEPORT   Q. Maniac raced it and won
___18. HYDRANT   R. Where Jeffrey was born
___19. EAST   S. Invited Maniac to his birthday party
___20. VOWELS   T. How Maniac felt at the end of the story
___21. TRAIN   U. The book Maniac wrote for Grayson: The Man Who Struck Out Willie ___
___22. THREE   V. End where the blacks lived
___23. HOLLIDAYSBURG   W. Jeffrey was afraid of losing it
___24. POLKAS   X. Where Maniac's aunt and uncle lived
___25. PILLBOX   Y. Jeffrey did this early in the morning, all over town

Maniac Magee Matching 1 Answer Key

L - 1. THOMPSON	A.	Taught Maniac to play baseball
A - 2. GRAYSON	B.	Star quarterback
W - 3. NAME	C.	Jeffrey kept his room clean
K - 4. FINSTERWALD	D.	Jeffrey's middle name
S - 5. PIPER	E.	These were hard for Grayson to learn
O - 6. PROTECTORS	F.	McNabs were building one in their living room
Y - 7. RAN	G.	Age when Jeffrey became an orphan
M - 8. MINORS	H.	Music Maniac and Grayson listened to
T - 9. CONTENT	I.	Someone used Amanda's book to make it
I - 10. CONFETTI	J.	Kids had a swimming party there: fire ___
N - 11. RUSSELL	K.	Scary house in East End
C - 12. MIRACLE	L.	Mars Bar's last name
P - 13. VALLEY	M.	Where Grayson played baseball
D - 14. LIONEL	N.	Stuck on the trolley trestle
B - 15. BRIAN	O.	Maniac slept on them: chest ___
U - 16. MAYS	P.	Maniac went to ___ Forge to wait for death
R - 17. BRIDGEPORT	Q.	Maniac raced it and won
J - 18. HYDRANT	R.	Where Jeffrey was born
V - 19. EAST	S.	Invited Maniac to his birthday party
E - 20. VOWELS	T.	How Maniac felt at the end of the story
Q - 21. TRAIN	U.	The book Maniac wrote for Grayson: The Man Who Struck Out Willie ___
G - 22. THREE	V.	End where the blacks lived
X - 23. HOLLIDAYSBURG	W.	Jeffrey was afraid of losing it
H - 24. POLKAS	X.	Where Maniac's aunt and uncle lived
F - 25. PILLBOX	Y.	Jeffrey did this early in the morning, all over town

Copyrighted

Maniac Magee Matching 2

___ 1. MIRACLE   A. Jeffrey's middle name
___ 2. MAYS   B. Where Maniac slept at first: ___ Park Zoo
___ 3. HECTOR   C. Where Jeffrey was born
___ 4. MINORS   D. Invited Maniac to his birthday party
___ 5. MULLIGAN   E. Amanda's 3 year old brother
___ 6. THOMPSON   F. Maniac lived there when he knew Grayson: ___ shell
___ 7. EAST   G. Someone used Amanda's book to make it
___ 8. PROTECTORS   H. Called Mars Bar IT
___ 9. GEORGE   I. Jeffrey kept his room clean
___ 10. CONFETTI   J. Maniac's real first name
___ 11. LESTER   K. Grayson lived there when he met Maniac
___ 12. YMCA   L. Maniac slept on them: chest ___
___ 13. HOLLIDAYSBURG   M. Amanda's 4 year old sister
___ 14. DUMP   N. The book Maniac wrote for Grayson: The Man Who Struck Out Willie ___
___ 15. JOHN   O. Mars Bar's last name
___ 16. THREE   P. Age when Jeffrey became an orphan
___ 17. ELMWOOD   Q. Amanda said Maniac could not get this card without an address
___ 18. HESTER   R. Largest player in the Little League
___ 19. BAND   S. Grayson's favorite book: Mike ___ and His Steam Shovel
___ 20. LIONEL   T. Where Grayson played baseball
___ 21. BUFFALO   U. End where the blacks lived
___ 22. BRIDGEPORT   V. Maniac walked barefoot through it
___ 23. LIBRARY   W. Where Maniac's aunt and uncle lived
___ 24. JEFFREY   X. Street that divided the East and West Ends
___ 25. PIPER   Y. Maniac kissed a baby one

Maniac Magee Matching 2 Answer Key

I - 1. MIRACLE	A. Jeffrey's middle name
N - 2. MAYS	B. Where Maniac slept at first: ___ Park Zoo
X - 3. HECTOR	C. Where Jeffrey was born
T - 4. MINORS	D. Invited Maniac to his birthday party
S - 5. MULLIGAN	E. Amanda's 3 year old brother
O - 6. THOMPSON	F. Maniac lived there when he knew Grayson: ___ shell
U - 7. EAST	G. Someone used Amanda's book to make it
L - 8. PROTECTORS	H. Called Mars Bar IT
H - 9. GEORGE	I. Jeffrey kept his room clean
G - 10. CONFETTI	J. Maniac's real first name
E - 11. LESTER	K. Grayson lived there when he met Maniac
K - 12. YMCA	L. Maniac slept on them: chest ___
W - 13. HOLLIDAYSBURG	M. Amanda's 4 year old sister
V - 14. DUMP	N. The book Maniac wrote for Grayson: The Man Who Struck Out Willie ___
R - 15. JOHN	O. Mars Bar's last name
P - 16. THREE	P. Age when Jeffrey became an orphan
B - 17. ELMWOOD	Q. Amanda said Maniac could not get this card without an address
M - 18. HESTER	R. Largest player in the Little League
F - 19. BAND	S. Grayson's favorite book: Mike ___ and His Steam Shovel
A - 20. LIONEL	T. Where Grayson played baseball
Y - 21. BUFFALO	U. End where the blacks lived
C - 22. BRIDGEPORT	V. Maniac walked barefoot through it
Q - 23. LIBRARY	W. Where Maniac's aunt and uncle lived
J - 24. JEFFREY	X. Street that divided the East and West Ends
D - 25. PIPER	Y. Maniac kissed a baby one

Copyrighted

Maniac Magee Matching 3

___ 1. PILLBOX   A. Where Jeffrey was born
___ 2. HECTOR   B. High school kids put him in Finsterwald's yard
___ 3. HOLLIDAYSBURG   C. Maniac took one every night with Hester and Lester
___ 4. JEFFREY   D. Stuck on the trolley trestle
___ 5. VALLEY   E. Jeffrey was afraid of losing it
___ 6. MARS   F. How Maniac felt at the end of the story
___ 7. CONTENT   G. McNabs were building one in their living room
___ 8. JOHN   H. Someone used Amanda's book to make it
___ 9. NAME   I. Went to the McNab house with Maniac: ___ Bar
___ 10. READ   J. Church where Manic went with the Beales
___ 11. HYDRANT   K. Maniac taught Grayson to do it
___ 12. EAST   L. Largest player in the Little League
___ 13. BRIDGEPORT   M. Maniac raced it and won
___ 14. BETHANY   N. The book Maniac wrote for Grayson: The Man Who Struck Out Willie ___
___ 15. MAYS   O. Made of string with lots of contortions: cobble's ___
___ 16. SCHUYLKILL   P. Where Maniac's aunt and uncle lived
___ 17. BATH   Q. Age when Jeffrey became an orphan
___ 18. THREE   R. End where the blacks lived
___ 19. CONFETTI   S. Maniac's real first name
___ 20. ARNOLD   T. Jeffrey's middle name
___ 21. RUSSELL   U. The trolley car fell off the track and into this river
___ 22. LIONEL   V. Maniac went to ___ Forge to wait for death
___ 23. KNOT   W. Kids had a swimming party there: fire ___
___ 24. VOWELS   X. These were hard for Grayson to learn
___ 25. TRAIN   Y. Street that divided the East and West Ends

Maniac Magee Matching 3 Answer Key

G - 1. PILLBOX		A. Where Jeffrey was born
Y - 2. HECTOR		B. High school kids put him in Finsterwald's yard
P - 3. HOLLIDAYSBURG		C. Maniac took one every night with Hester and Lester
S - 4. JEFFREY		D. Stuck on the trolley trestle
V - 5. VALLEY		E. Jeffrey was afraid of losing it
I - 6. MARS		F. How Maniac felt at the end of the story
F - 7. CONTENT		G. McNabs were building one in their living room
L - 8. JOHN		H. Someone used Amanda's book to make it
E - 9. NAME		I. Went to the McNab house with Maniac: ___ Bar
K - 10. READ		J. Church where Manic went with the Beales
W - 11. HYDRANT		K. Maniac taught Grayson to do it
R - 12. EAST		L. Largest player in the Little League
A - 13. BRIDGEPORT		M. Maniac raced it and won
J - 14. BETHANY		N. The book Maniac wrote for Grayson: The Man Who Struck Out Willie ___
N - 15. MAYS		O. Made of string with lots of contortions: cobble's ___
U - 16. SCHUYLKILL		P. Where Maniac's aunt and uncle lived
C - 17. BATH		Q. Age when Jeffrey became an orphan
Q - 18. THREE		R. End where the blacks lived
H - 19. CONFETTI		S. Maniac's real first name
B - 20. ARNOLD		T. Jeffrey's middle name
D - 21. RUSSELL		U. The trolley car fell off the track and into this river
T - 22. LIONEL		V. Maniac went to ___ Forge to wait for death
O - 23. KNOT		W. Kids had a swimming party there: fire ___
X - 24. VOWELS		X. These were hard for Grayson to learn
M - 25. TRAIN		Y. Street that divided the East and West Ends

Maniac Magee Matching 4

___ 1. PROTECTORS   A. Jeffrey's middle name
___ 2. LIBRARY   B. Amanda said Maniac could not get this card without an address
___ 3. READ   C. The trolley car fell off the track and into this river
___ 4. THREE   D. Age when Jeffrey became an orphan
___ 5. CONSONANTS   E. Mars Bar's last name
___ 6. GRAYSON   F. The book Maniac wrote for Grayson: The Man Who Struck Out Willie ___
___ 7. CRUSADE   G. Taught Maniac to play baseball
___ 8. JOHN   H. The Beale family lived on this street
___ 9. SYCAMORE   I. Title of book Maniac borrowed from Amanda: Children's ___
___ 10. MAYS   J. Jeffrey was afraid of losing it
___ 11. LESTER   K. Maniac taught Grayson to do it
___ 12. VOWELS   L. Jeffrey did it during the concert
___ 13. SCHUYLKILL   M. Easy for Grayson to learn
___ 14. DUMP   N. Grayson's favorite book: Mike ___ and His Steam Shovel
___ 15. SCREAM   O. Largest player in the Little League
___ 16. BRIDGEPORT   P. Maniac took one every night with Hester and Lester
___ 17. MIRACLE   Q. Where Jeffrey was born
___ 18. NAME   R. These were hard for Grayson to learn
___ 19. PIZZA   S. Russell was stuck on it
___ 20. BATH   T. Maniac was allergic to it
___ 21. TRESTLE   U. Amanda's 3 year old brother
___ 22. THOMPSON   V. Church where Manic went with the Beales
___ 23. BETHANY   W. Maniac slept on them: chest ___
___ 24. LIONEL   X. Maniac walked barefoot through it
___ 25. MULLIGAN   Y. Jeffrey kept his room clean

Maniac Magee Matching 4 Answer Key

W - 1.	PROTECTORS	A. Jeffrey's middle name
B - 2.	LIBRARY	B. Amanda said Maniac could not get this card without an address
K - 3.	READ	C. The trolley car fell off the track and into this river
D - 4.	THREE	D. Age when Jeffrey became an orphan
M - 5.	CONSONANTS	E. Mars Bar's last name
G - 6.	GRAYSON	F. The book Maniac wrote for Grayson: The Man Who Struck Out Willie ___
I - 7.	CRUSADE	G. Taught Maniac to play baseball
O - 8.	JOHN	H. The Beale family lived on this street
H - 9.	SYCAMORE	I. Title of book Maniac borrowed from Amanda: Children's ___
F - 10.	MAYS	J. Jeffrey was afraid of losing it
U - 11.	LESTER	K. Maniac taught Grayson to do it
R - 12.	VOWELS	L. Jeffrey did it during the concert
C - 13.	SCHUYLKILL	M. Easy for Grayson to learn
X - 14.	DUMP	N. Grayson's favorite book: Mike ___ and His Steam Shovel
L - 15.	SCREAM	O. Largest player in the Little League
Q - 16.	BRIDGEPORT	P. Maniac took one every night with Hester and Lester
Y - 17.	MIRACLE	Q. Where Jeffrey was born
J - 18.	NAME	R. These were hard for Grayson to learn
T - 19.	PIZZA	S. Russell was stuck on it
P - 20.	BATH	T. Maniac was allergic to it
S - 21.	TRESTLE	U. Amanda's 3 year old brother
E - 22.	THOMPSON	V. Church where Manic went with the Beales
V - 23.	BETHANY	W. Maniac slept on them: chest ___
A - 24.	LIONEL	X. Maniac walked barefoot through it
N - 25.	MULLIGAN	Y. Jeffrey kept his room clean

Maniac Magee Magic Squares 1

Match the definition with the vocabulary word. Put your answers in the magic squares below. When your answers are correct, all columns and rows will add to the same number.

A. MULLIGAN
B. PIPER
C. PITCHER
D. MAYS
E. CONFETTI
F. THREE
G. BUFFALO
H. HANDS
I. HYDRANT
J. JEFFREY
K. BETHANY
L. TRAIN
M. MILLS
N. PILLBOX
O. AMANDA
P. HESTER

1. She had a suitcase full of books
2. The book Maniac wrote for Grayson: The Man Who Struck Out Willie ___
3. Maniac's real first name
4. Someone used Amanda's book to make it
5. Kids had a swimming party there: fire ___
6. Age when Jeffrey became an orphan
7. Amanda's 4 year old sister
8. Grayson's position
9. Receiver doing a fly pattern: ___ down
10. Church where Manic went with the Beales
11. Grayson's favorite book: Mike ___ and His Steam Shovel
12. McNabs were building one in their living room
13. Invited Maniac to his birthday party
14. Where Jeffrey ended up: Two ___
15. Maniac kissed a baby one
16. Maniac raced it and won

A=	B=	C=	D=
E=	F=	G=	H=
I=	J=	K=	L=
M=	N=	O=	P=

Maniac Magee Magic Squares 1 Answer Key

Match the definition with the vocabulary word. Put your answers in the magic squares below. When your answers are correct, all columns and rows will add to the same number.

A. MULLIGAN
B. PIPER
C. PITCHER
D. MAYS
E. CONFETTI
F. THREE
G. BUFFALO
H. HANDS
I. HYDRANT
J. JEFFREY
K. BETHANY
L. TRAIN
M. MILLS
N. PILLBOX
O. AMANDA
P. HESTER

1. She had a suitcase full of books
2. The book Maniac wrote for Grayson: The Man Who Struck Out Willie ___
3. Maniac's real first name
4. Someone used Amanda's book to make it
5. Kids had a swimming party there: fire ___
6. Age when Jeffrey became an orphan
7. Amanda's 4 year old sister
8. Grayson's position
9. Receiver doing a fly pattern: ___ down
10. Church where Manic went with the Beales
11. Grayson's favorite book: Mike ___ and His Steam Shovel
12. McNabs were building one in their living room
13. Invited Maniac to his birthday party
14. Where Jeffrey ended up: Two ___
15. Maniac kissed a baby one
16. Maniac raced it and won

A=11	B=13	C=8	D=2
E=4	F=6	G=15	H=9
I=5	J=3	K=10	L=16
M=14	N=12	O=1	P=7

Maniac Magee Magic Squares 2

Match the definition with the vocabulary word. Put your answers in the magic squares below. When your answers are correct, all columns and rows will add to the same number.

A. BATH
B. SCHUYLKILL
C. HANDS
D. EAST
E. JOHN
F. MIRACLE
G. POLKAS
H. DOT
I. COBRAS
J. LESTER
K. PIZZA
L. DAN
M. SNICKERS
N. PROTECTORS
O. TRESTLE
P. PIPER

1. Aunt ___ hated her husband
2. Maniac took one every night with Hester and Lester
3. The trolley car fell off the track and into this river
4. Music Maniac and Grayson listened to
5. Amanda's 3 year old brother
6. Russell was stuck on it
7. Invited Maniac to his birthday party
8. McNab's group of friends
9. Maniac was allergic to it
10. Maniac slept on them: chest ___
11. Amanda said she was changing Mars Bar's name to this
12. Uncle __ didn't talk to his wife
13. Largest player in the Little League
14. End where the blacks lived
15. Receiver doing a fly pattern: ___ down
16. Jeffrey kept his room clean

A=	B=	C=	D=
E=	F=	G=	H=
I=	J=	K=	L=
M=	N=	O=	P=

Maniac Magee Magic Squares 2 Answer Key

Match the definition with the vocabulary word. Put your answers in the magic squares below. When your answers are correct, all columns and rows will add to the same number.

A. BATH
B. SCHUYLKILL
C. HANDS
D. EAST
E. JOHN
F. MIRACLE
G. POLKAS
H. DOT
I. COBRAS
J. LESTER
K. PIZZA
L. DAN
M. SNICKERS
N. PROTECTORS
O. TRESTLE
P. PIPER

1. Aunt ___ hated her husband
2. Maniac took one every night with Hester and Lester
3. The trolley car fell off the track and into this river
4. Music Maniac and Grayson listened to
5. Amanda's 3 year old brother
6. Russell was stuck on it
7. Invited Maniac to his birthday party
8. McNab's group of friends
9. Maniac was allergic to it
10. Maniac slept on them: chest ___
11. Amanda said she was changing Mars Bar's name to this
12. Uncle __ didn't talk to his wife
13. Largest player in the Little League
14. End where the blacks lived
15. Receiver doing a fly pattern: ___ down
16. Jeffrey kept his room clean

A=2	B=3	C=15	D=14
E=13	F=16	G=4	H=1
I=8	J=5	K=9	L=12
M=11	N=10	O=6	P=7

Maniac Magee Magic Squares 3

Match the definition with the vocabulary word. Put your answers in the magic squares below. When your answers are correct, all columns and rows will add to the same number.

A. BAND
B. HYDRANT
C. GEORGE
D. FROGBALL
E. PIZZA
F. MULLIGAN
G. PITCHER
H. BUFFALO
I. HECTOR
J. YMCA
K. DAN
L. BRIAN
M. CONTENT
N. AMANDA
O. JOHN
P. GRAYSON

1. Maniac kissed a baby one
2. How Maniac felt at the end of the story
3. Kids had a swimming party there: fire ___
4. Uncle ___ didn't talk to his wife
5. Grayson lived there when he met Maniac
6. Called Mars Bar IT
7. Taught Maniac to play baseball
8. Maniac was allergic to it
9. Largest player in the Little League
10. Grayson's favorite book: Mike ___ and His Steam Shovel
11. Street that divided the East and West Ends
12. Maniac logged the world's first one
13. Maniac lived there when he knew Grayson: ___ shell
14. Star quarterback
15. Grayson's position
16. She had a suitcase full of books

A=	B=	C=	D=
E=	F=	G=	H=
I=	J=	K=	L=
M=	N=	O=	P=

Maniac Magee Magic Squares 3 Answer Key

Match the definition with the vocabulary word. Put your answers in the magic squares below. When your answers are correct, all columns and rows will add to the same number.

A. BAND
B. HYDRANT
C. GEORGE
D. FROGBALL
E. PIZZA
F. MULLIGAN
G. PITCHER
H. BUFFALO
I. HECTOR
J. YMCA
K. DAN
L. BRIAN
M. CONTENT
N. AMANDA
O. JOHN
P. GRAYSON

1. Maniac kissed a baby one
2. How Maniac felt at the end of the story
3. Kids had a swimming party there: fire ___
4. Uncle ___ didn't talk to his wife
5. Grayson lived there when he met Maniac
6. Called Mars Bar IT
7. Taught Maniac to play baseball
8. Maniac was allergic to it
9. Largest player in the Little League
10. Grayson's favorite book: Mike ___ and His Steam Shovel
11. Street that divided the East and West Ends
12. Maniac logged the world's first one
13. Maniac lived there when he knew Grayson: ___ shell
14. Star quarterback
15. Grayson's position
16. She had a suitcase full of books

A=13	B=3	C=6	D=12
E=8	F=10	G=15	H=1
I=11	J=5	K=4	L=14
M=2	N=16	O=9	P=7

Maniac Magee Magic Squares 4

Match the definition with the vocabulary word. Put your answers in the magic squares below. When your answers are correct, all columns and rows will add to the same number.

A. PIZZA
B. TRASH
C. ELMWOOD
D. LESTER
E. CONTENT
F. JOHN
G. SNICKERS
H. READ
I. EAST
J. COULD
K. FROGBALL
L. BRIAN
M. LIBRARY
N. VOWELS
O. RAN
P. CRUSADE

1. Mrs. Beale didn't want Maniac using this kind of talk in her house
2. Amanda said she was changing Mars Bar's name to this
3. Maniac logged the world's first one
4. These were hard for Grayson to learn
5. Amanda said Maniac could not get this card without an address
6. Star quarterback
7. Maniac taught Grayson to do it
8. Maniac was allergic to it
9. Title of book Maniac borrowed from Amanda: Children's ___
10. End where the blacks lived
11. How Maniac felt at the end of the story
12. Amanda's 3 year old brother
13. Where Maniac slept at first: ___ Park Zoo
14. Largest player in the Little League
15. First book Grayson read: The Little Engine That ___
16. Jeffrey did this early in the morning, all over town

A=	B=	C=	D=
E=	F=	G=	H=
I=	J=	K=	L=
M=	N=	O=	P=

Maniac Magee Magic Squares 4 Answer Key

Match the definition with the vocabulary word. Put your answers in the magic squares below. When your answers are correct, all columns and rows will add to the same number.

A. PIZZA
B. TRASH
C. ELMWOOD
D. LESTER
E. CONTENT
F. JOHN
G. SNICKERS
H. READ
I. EAST
J. COULD
K. FROGBALL
L. BRIAN
M. LIBRARY
N. VOWELS
O. RAN
P. CRUSADE

1. Mrs. Beale didn't want Maniac using this kind of talk in her house
2. Amanda said she was changing Mars Bar's name to this
3. Maniac logged the world's first one
4. These were hard for Grayson to learn
5. Amanda said Maniac could not get this card without an address
6. Star quarterback
7. Maniac taught Grayson to do it
8. Maniac was allergic to it
9. Title of book Maniac borrowed from Amanda: Children's ___
10. End where the blacks lived
11. How Maniac felt at the end of the story
12. Amanda's 3 year old brother
13. Where Maniac slept at first: ___ Park Zoo
14. Largest player in the Little League
15. First book Grayson read: The Little Engine That ___
16. Jeffrey did this early in the morning, all over town

A=8	B=1	C=13	D=12
E=11	F=14	G=2	H=7
I=10	J=15	K=3	L=6
M=5	N=4	O=16	P=9

Maniac Magee Word Search 1

```
E V O L G P I T C H E R B K X C N J
L A H Y R C T R A I N E U J H O A J
C E S W U R H O J N L P F C S N D J
A L Y T B U R P G Y H I F Y S T H S
R M C P S S E E S S X P A Q S E E H
I W A I Y A E G B C N R L G P N S F
M O M Z A D D D R R G I O J R T T T
D O O Z D E U I G E I K C T O W E V
J D R A I C M R C A A J K T Q R Y
D H E M L G P B V M P D N D E T N Y
S Y H I L E N O I L Y X D Y C R N M
T D S N O C W Y Q E B R E S T E S R
J R Y O H E E D L O N R A M O S E X
J A A R L X M L Q F F R M K R T Y Y
O N M S D N A H N F B A N D S L M Z
H T V K H V N A E O R O C E O E C R
N B A T H Z R J C S T G L P V T A T
```

Age when Jeffrey became an orphan (5)
Amanda said she was changing Mars Bar's name to this (8)
Amanda's 3 year old brother (6)
Amanda's 4 year old sister (6)
Aunt ___ hated her husband (3)
End where the blacks lived (4)
Grayson lived there when he met Maniac (4)
Grayson's Christmas present to Maniac (5)
Grayson's position (7)
High school kids put him in Finsterwald's yard (6)
How Maniac felt at the end of the story (7)
Invited Maniac to his birthday party (5)
Jeffrey did it during the concert (6)
Jeffrey did this early in the morning, all over town (3)
Jeffrey kept his room clean (7)
Jeffrey was afraid of losing it (4)
Jeffrey's middle name (6)
Kids had a swimming party there: fire ___ (7)
Largest player in the Little League (4)
Made of string with lots of contortions: cobble's ___ (4)
Maniac kissed a baby one (7)
Maniac lived there when he knew Grayson: ___ shell (4)
Maniac raced it and won (5)
Maniac slept on them: chest ___ (10)
Maniac taught Grayson to do it (4)
Maniac took one every night with Hester and Lester (4)
Maniac walked barefoot through it (4)
Maniac was allergic to it (5)
Maniac went to ___ Forge to wait for death (6)
Maniac's real first name (7)
McNab's group of friends (6)
Mrs. Beale didn't want Maniac using this kind of talk in her house (5)
Receiver doing a fly pattern: ___ down (5)
Russell was stuck on it (7)
Star quarterback (5)
Taught Maniac to play baseball (7)
The Beale family lived on this street (8)
The book Maniac wrote for Grayson: The Man Who Struck Out Willie ___ (4)
These were hard for Grayson to learn (6)
Title of book Maniac borrowed from Amanda: Children's ___ (7)
Uncle ___ didn't talk to his wife (3)
Went to the McNab house with Maniac: ___ Bar (4)
Where Grayson played baseball (6)
Where Jeffrey was born (10)
Where Maniac slept at first: ___ Park Zoo (7)
Where Maniac's aunt and uncle lived (13)

Maniac Magee Word Search 1 Answer Key

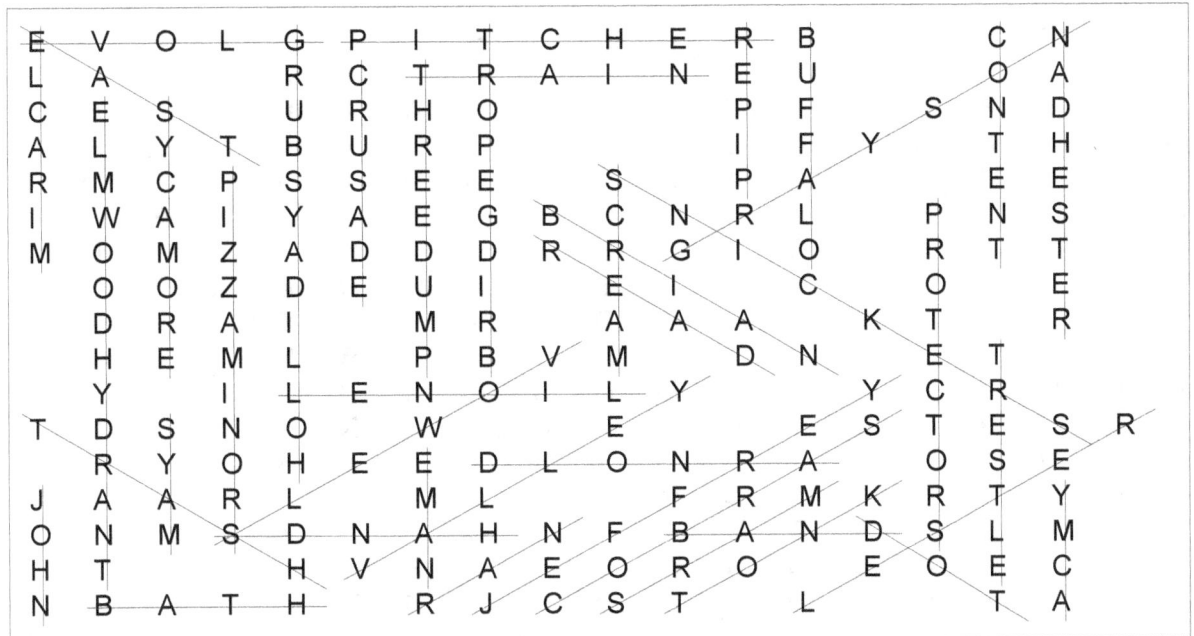

Age when Jeffrey became an orphan (5)
Amanda said she was changing Mars Bar's name to this (8)
Amanda's 3 year old brother (6)
Amanda's 4 year old sister (6)
Aunt ___ hated her husband (3)
End where the blacks lived (4)
Grayson lived there when he met Maniac (4)
Grayson's Christmas present to Maniac (5)
Grayson's position (7)
High school kids put him in Finsterwald's yard (6)
How Maniac felt at the end of the story (7)
Invited Maniac to his birthday party (5)
Jeffrey did it during the concert (6)
Jeffrey did this early in the morning, all over town (3)
Jeffrey kept his room clean (7)
Jeffrey was afraid of losing it (4)
Jeffrey's middle name (6)
Kids had a swimming party there: fire ___ (7)
Largest player in the Little League (4)
Made of string with lots of contortions: cobble's ___ (4)
Maniac kissed a baby one (7)
Maniac lived there when he knew Grayson: ___ shell (4)
Maniac raced it and won (5)
Maniac slept on them: chest ___ (10)
Maniac taught Grayson to do it (4)
Maniac took one every night with Hester and Lester (4)
Maniac walked barefoot through it (4)
Maniac was allergic to it (5)
Maniac went to ___ Forge to wait for death (6)
Maniac's real first name (7)
McNab's group of friends (6)
Mrs. Beale didn't want Maniac using this kind of talk in her house (5)
Receiver doing a fly pattern: ___ down (5)
Russell was stuck on it (7)
Star quarterback (5)
Taught Maniac to play baseball (7)
The Beale family lived on this street (8)
The book Maniac wrote for Grayson: The Man Who Struck Out Willie ___ (4)
These were hard for Grayson to learn (6)
Title of book Maniac borrowed from Amanda: Children's ___ (7)
Uncle __ didn't talk to his wife (3)
Went to the McNab house with Maniac: ___ Bar (4)
Where Grayson played baseball (6)
Where Jeffrey was born (10)
Where Maniac slept at first: ___ Park Zoo (7)
Where Maniac's aunt and uncle lived (13)

Maniac Magee Word Search 2

```
G L O V E M I N O R S B H G J C P L
V E M H E S T E R C L R B R E O I Z
P L I B R A R Y P Y E I A A F B P Q
M M L N H P I Z Z A W D T Y F R E F
R W L C T T R A I N O G H S R A R W
F O S L N P C O D R V E V O E S H R
P O V H E K O M T K K P L N Y E A Q
O D W E T H N T F E Y O F R M A N Q
L V O C N H S R R D C R E A F S D Z
K N O T O T O Y N A H T E B N T S B
A C G O C G N M M N S R O H A Y S H
S Z M R B B A A P E C H O R A N Z R
B S Q A C D N R L S N J D M S T D W
D R L Z R D T C N X O B L L I P A N
C L I D A S S D X O G N N G K C F C
X M J A N C O U L D Q F W M G W Z
D U M P N A M E Z H L D H Y R E A D
```

Age when Jeffrey became an orphan (5)
Amanda said Maniac could not get this card without an address (7)
Amanda's 3 year old brother (6)
Amanda's 4 year old sister (6)
Aunt ___ hated her husband (3)
Church where Manic went with the Beales (7)
Easy for Grayson to learn (10)
End where the blacks lived (4)
First book Grayson read: The Little Engine That ___ (5)
Grayson lived there when he met Maniac (4)
Grayson's Christmas present to Maniac (5)
High school kids put him in Finsterwald's yard (6)
How Maniac felt at the end of the story (7)
Invited Maniac to his birthday party (5)
Jeffrey did it during the concert (6)
Jeffrey did this early in the morning, all over town (3)
Jeffrey was afraid of losing it (4)
Largest player in the Little League (4)
Made of string with lots of contortions: cobble's ___ (4)
Maniac lived there when he knew Grayson: ___ shell (4)
Maniac logged the world's first one (8)
Maniac raced it and won (5)
Maniac slept on them: chest ___ (10)
Maniac taught Grayson to do it (4)
Maniac took one every night with Hester and Lester (4)
Maniac walked barefoot through it (4)
Maniac was allergic to it (5)
Maniac's real first name (7)
Mars Bar's last name (8)
McNab's group of friends (6)
McNabs were building one in their living room (7)
Mrs. Beale didn't want Maniac using this kind of talk in her house (5)
Music Maniac and Grayson listened to (6)
Receiver doing a fly pattern: ___ down (5)
She had a suitcase full of books (6)
Star quarterback (5)
Street that divided the East and West Ends (6)
Taught Maniac to play baseball (7)
The book Maniac wrote for Grayson: The Man Who Struck Out Willie ___ (4)
These were hard for Grayson to learn (6)
Uncle __ didn't talk to his wife (3)
Went to the McNab house with Maniac: ___ Bar (4)
Where Grayson played baseball (6)
Where Jeffrey ended up: Two ___ (5)
Where Jeffrey was born (10)
Where Maniac slept at first: ___ Park Zoo (7)

Maniac Magee Word Search 2 Answer Key

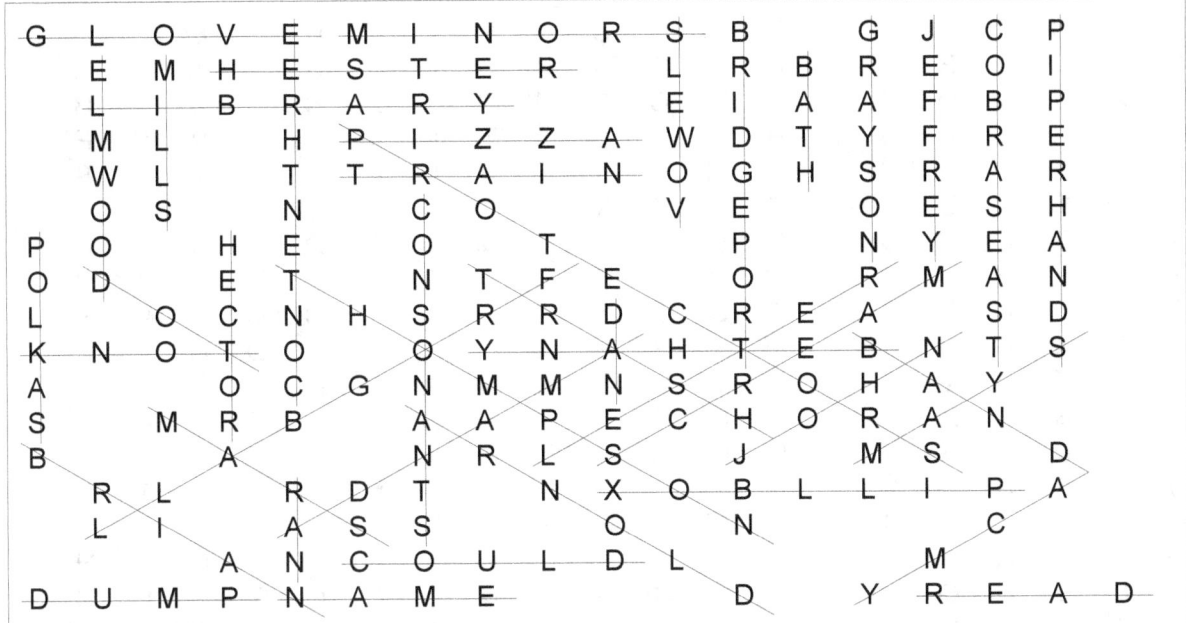

Age when Jeffrey became an orphan (5)
Amanda said Maniac could not get this card without an address (7)
Amanda's 3 year old brother (6)
Amanda's 4 year old sister (6)
Aunt ___ hated her husband (3)
Church where Manic went with the Beales (7)
Easy for Grayson to learn (10)
End where the blacks lived (4)
First book Grayson read: The Little Engine That ___ (5)
Grayson lived there when he met Maniac (4)
Grayson's Christmas present to Maniac (5)
High school kids put him in Finsterwald's yard (6)
How Maniac felt at the end of the story (7)
Invited Maniac to his birthday party (5)
Jeffrey did it during the concert (6)
Jeffrey did this early in the morning, all over town (3)
Jeffrey was afraid of losing it (4)
Largest player in the Little League (4)
Made of string with lots of contortions: cobble's ___ (4)
Maniac lived there when he knew Grayson: ___ shell (4)
Maniac logged the world's first one (8)
Maniac raced it and won (5)
Maniac slept on them: chest ___ (10)

Maniac taught Grayson to do it (4)
Maniac took one every night with Hester and Lester (4)
Maniac walked barefoot through it (4)
Maniac was allergic to it (5)
Maniac's real first name (7)
Mars Bar's last name (8)
McNab's group of friends (6)
McNabs were building one in their living room (7)
Mrs. Beale didn't want Maniac using this kind of talk in her house (5)
Music Maniac and Grayson listened to (6)
Receiver doing a fly pattern: ___ down (5)
She had a suitcase full of books (6)
Star quarterback (5)
Street that divided the East and West Ends (6)
Taught Maniac to play baseball (7)
The book Maniac wrote for Grayson: The Man Who Struck Out Willie ___ (4)
These were hard for Grayson to learn (6)
Uncle __ didn't talk to his wife (3)
Went to the McNab house with Maniac: ___ Bar (4)
Where Grayson played baseball (6)
Where Jeffrey ended up: Two ___ (5)
Where Jeffrey was born (10)
Where Maniac slept at first: ___ Park Zoo (7)

Maniac Magee Word Search 3

```
H A N D S L L E W K C I P I T C H E R N
O G Q R E A B E N D S D B I O S T K E R
L Z V M D R M R V C O W R N Z B K D T R B
L G A B A N D H K N O T T M M Z A V S E F
I N E M S O D T M L R E H U I E A T E S
D M F O U L L T A K N F O L R C L C H K
A I D K R D T F E T K R M L A D N A M A
Y N L R C G F M R R C O P I C H U G K W
S O F I M U E T C S O G S G L C C M W S
B R K M B Y O S S N B O A E L D H P C
U S T P L R B P Y L S A N N S L S Z V R
R Q R E Z R A C F P O L M N A A F S P W
G P E T A M A R N O N L L W R O T C E H
V Q S S P M V G Y L A D R T M T R H T T
O W T J O B A L L K N E N F N B Z R S T
W B L R V Q L H E A T G A A R R A E N H
E L E N O I L L E S S U R E P I P A I H
L Z H T Y M E D N D T D Q A N A D S C W
S O W R H J Y I D Y Y E N Y N L T K K
J G B R G A F N P H D L R M L S U Y E Z
G L O V E H N D A N M A R S C T O N R J
E L M W O O D Y M A Y S G S Z A C N S D
```

AMANDA	EAST	LESTER	RAN
ARNOLD	ELMWOOD	LIBRARY	READ
BAND	FINSTERWALD	LIONEL	RUSSELL
BATH	FROGBALL	MARS	SCREAM
BETHANY	GEORGE	MAYS	SNICKERS
BRIAN	GLOVE	MILLS	SYCAMORE
BUFFALO	GRAYSON	MINORS	THOMPSON
COBRAS	HANDS	MIRACLE	THREE
CONSONANTS	HECTOR	MULLIGAN	TRAIN
CONTENT	HESTER	NAME	TRASH
COULD	HOLLIDAYSBURG	PICKWELLS	TRESTLE
CRUSADE	HYDRANT	PIPER	VALLEY
DAN	JOHN	PITCHER	VOWELS
DOT	KNOT	PIZZA	YMCA
DUMP	KRIMPETS	POLKAS	

Maniac Magee Word Search 3 Answer Key

```
H A N D S L L E W K C I P I T C H E R
O     E A   E   D       I O       R
L     M D   R       O   N Z   B D T
L   G A B A N D H K N O T M M Z A   S
I   N E   S O   T M L   E H U I E T E
D   M   O U L     A     N F O L A   H
A     I   K R D F E T   F R M L D N A M A
Y     N L R C G F E R   C O P I C U
S     O   I U E   C   O N G S G L   M
B     R   M B   O S S   N B O A E L D H P
U     S T   P   R B   Y   S A   N     L S
R       R E   R A C   P   O L         A
G       E T   A A R   O   N L     W R O T C E H
V       S S   M V   Y L   A R T   T         T
O       T     O A L   K E N   N B   R     S
W   B   L R     L   E A T G A A   R A   N
E   L   N O I L L E S S U R E P I P A   I
L   I   T     E     N T D   A N S   S   C
S   O         Y I   N     Y E Y Y   S T   K
J           A F   H   R M     U L   E
G L O V E     N D A N M A R S C     O     R
E L M W O O D Y M A Y S           A C   N S
```

AMANDA	EAST	LESTER	RAN
ARNOLD	ELMWOOD	LIBRARY	READ
BAND	FINSTERWALD	LIONEL	RUSSELL
BATH	FROGBALL	MARS	SCREAM
BETHANY	GEORGE	MAYS	SNICKERS
BRIAN	GLOVE	MILLS	SYCAMORE
BUFFALO	GRAYSON	MINORS	THOMPSON
COBRAS	HANDS	MIRACLE	THREE
CONSONANTS	HECTOR	MULLIGAN	TRAIN
CONTENT	HESTER	NAME	TRASH
COULD	HOLLIDAYSBURG	PICKWELLS	TRESTLE
CRUSADE	HYDRANT	PIPER	VALLEY
DAN	JOHN	PITCHER	VOWELS
DOT	KNOT	PIZZA	YMCA
DUMP	KRIMPETS	POLKAS	

Maniac Magee Word Search 4

```
Y Z M Q X S B L S X Q S N Y S S F P J M
W W I S A H U S D C D B I L M L E I D Z
G D L K J M F R N N Y D A S K C D L D R
V A L L E Y F N A I A F R O G B A L L V
V O S E F N A B H N C O T D R W S B O Y
P G W B S I L L X M N K L A R P U O N E
C B S E R T O Z I I A E E E Q R R X R Q
Y C E B L I E T M B N Y T R S R C O A K
S S M T T S D R H O R S S R S O M C S V
K T A N H J N G I O N A A Y U A E O C L
N N N G R A E L E I M R L C D L N R W
B A T H E K N F F P X P D Y N O M F E B
G N Y H E O N Y F V O S S O R T W E A D
D O K R A G R O R R L R S O J T O T M H
H S P F M T P G T Z E Y T H N X O T H T
C N T S A E I L E X A Y C E E E D I E M
K O P B N S Z H K R S N T O L C D J S D
Q C H R D B Z H G C N N R C B W T Z T H
J O H N A U A K Q L O Y A V Q R M O E W
P I P E R C M Y M C O R S M W M A V R G
H Y D R A N T P G L I V H B K J M S K S
R U S S E L L C Z M T R E S T L E S C Q
```

AMANDA	COULD	HANDS	MILLS	SNICKERS
ARNOLD	CRUSADE	HECTOR	MINORS	SYCAMORE
BAND	DAN	HESTER	MIRACLE	THOMPSON
BATH	DOT	HYDRANT	NAME	THREE
BETHANY	DUMP	JEFFREY	PILLBOX	TRAIN
BRIAN	EAST	JOHN	PIPER	TRASH
BRIDGEPORT	ELMWOOD	KNOT	PIZZA	TRESTLE
BUFFALO	FINSTERWALD	LESTER	POLKAS	VALLEY
COBRAS	FROGBALL	LIBRARY	RAN	VOWELS
CONFETTI	GEORGE	LIONEL	READ	YMCA
CONSONANTS	GLOVE	MARS	RUSSELL	
CONTENT	GRAYSON	MAYS	SCREAM	

Maniac Magee Word Search 4 Answer Key

AMANDA	COULD	HANDS	MILLS	SNICKERS
ARNOLD	CRUSADE	HECTOR	MINORS	SYCAMORE
BAND	DAN	HESTER	MIRACLE	THOMPSON
BATH	DOT	HYDRANT	NAME	THREE
BETHANY	DUMP	JEFFREY	PILLBOX	TRAIN
BRIAN	EAST	JOHN	PIPER	TRASH
BRIDGEPORT	ELMWOOD	KNOT	PIZZA	TRESTLE
BUFFALO	FINSTERWALD	LESTER	POLKAS	VALLEY
COBRAS	FROGBALL	LIBRARY	RAN	VOWELS
CONFETTI	GEORGE	LIONEL	READ	YMCA
CONSONANTS	GLOVE	MARS	RUSSELL	
CONTENT	GRAYSON	MAYS	SCREAM	

Maniac Magee Crossword 1

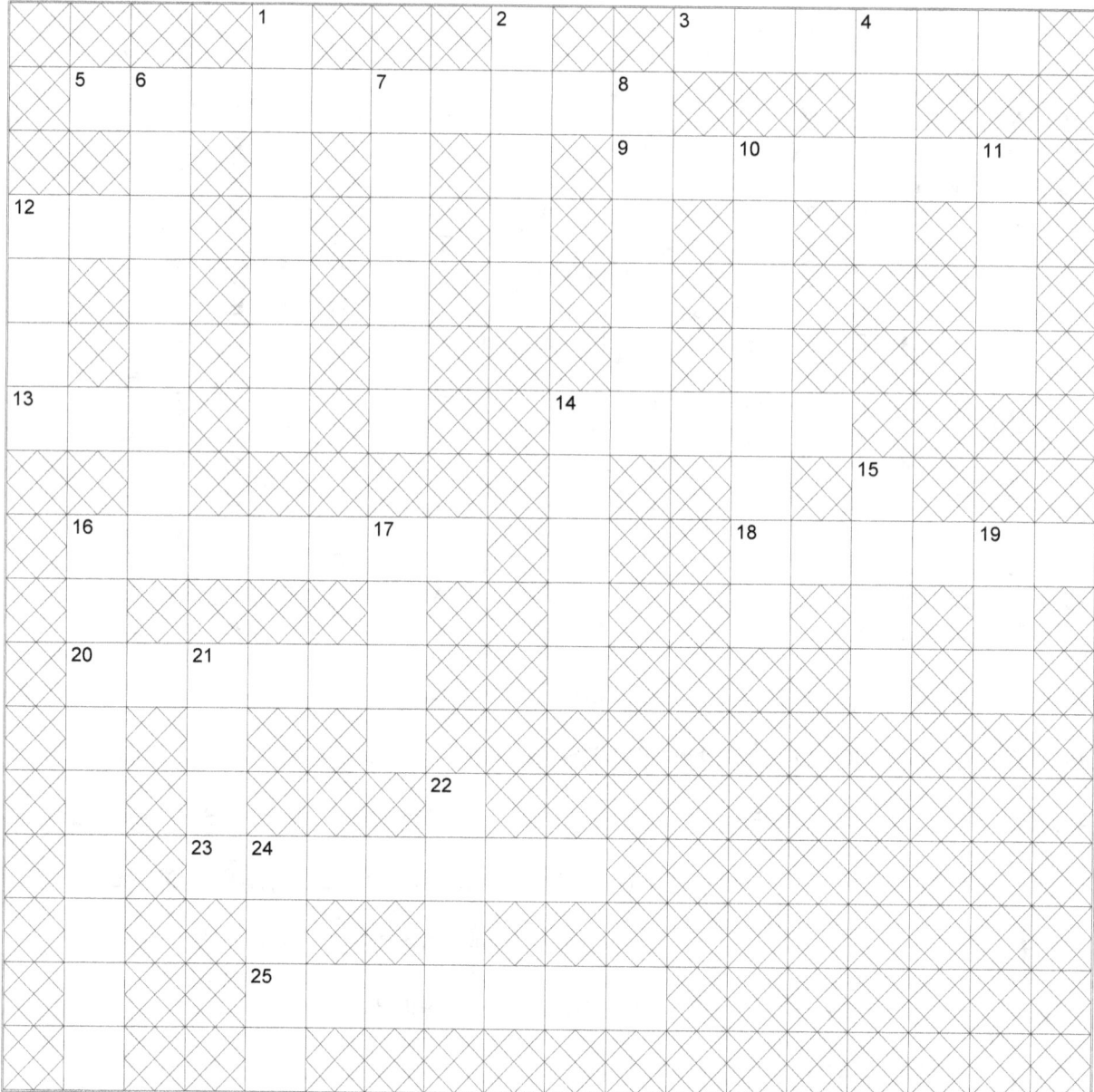

Across

3. Music Maniac and Grayson listened to
5. The trolley car fell off the track and into this river
9. Where Maniac slept at first: ___ Park Zoo
12. Jeffrey did this early in the morning, all over town
13. Aunt ___ hated her husband
14. Maniac raced it and won
16. Grayson's position
18. She had a suitcase full of books
20. McNab's group of friends
23. Kids had a swimming party there: fire ___
25. Title of book Maniac borrowed from Amanda: Children's ___

Down

1. Maniac kissed a baby one
2. Invited Maniac to his birthday party
4. Made of string with lots of contortions: cobble's ___
6. Someone used Amanda's book to make it
7. Jeffrey's middle name
8. Amanda's 3 year old brother
10. Grayson's favorite book: Mike ___ and His Steam Shovel
11. Maniac walked barefoot through it
12. Maniac taught Grayson to do it
14. Age when Jeffrey became an orphan
15. Maniac lived there when he knew Grayson: ___ shell
16. Maniac and Mars Bar ate dinner with them
17. End where the blacks lived
19. Uncle __ didn't talk to his wife
21. Maniac took one every night with Hester and Lester
22. The book Maniac wrote for Grayson: The Man Who Struck Out Willie ___
24. Grayson lived there when he met Maniac

Maniac Magee Crossword 1 Answer Key

			1 B		2 P		3 P	O	L	4 K	A	S
	5 S	6 C	H	U	Y	7 L	K	I	8 L	L		N	
		O		F	I		P	9 E	L	10 M	W	O	11 D
12 R	A	N		F	O	E		S		U		T		U
E		F		A	N	R		T		L				M
A		E		L	E			E		L				P
13 D	O	T		O	L		14 T	R	A	I	N			
		T					H			G		15 B	
	16 P	I	T	C	17 H	E	R			18 A	M	A	19 N	D	A
	I				A		E			N		N		A
	20 C	O	21 B	R	A	S		E				D		N
	K		A											
	W		T			22 M							
	E		23 H	24 Y	D	R	A	N	T			
	L			M		Y						
	L		25 C	R	U	S	A	D	E		
	S			A							

Across
- 3. Music Maniac and Grayson listened to
- 5. The trolley car fell off the track and into this river
- 9. Where Maniac slept at first: ___ Park Zoo
- 12. Jeffrey did this early in the morning, all over town
- 13. Aunt ___ hated her husband
- 14. Maniac raced it and won
- 16. Grayson's position
- 18. She had a suitcase full of books
- 20. McNab's group of friends
- 23. Kids had a swimming party there: fire ___
- 25. Title of book Maniac borrowed from Amanda: Children's ___

Down
- 1. Maniac kissed a baby one
- 2. Invited Maniac to his birthday party
- 4. Made of string with lots of contortions: cobble's ___
- 6. Someone used Amanda's book to make it
- 7. Jeffrey's middle name
- 8. Amanda's 3 year old brother
- 10. Grayson's favorite book: Mike ___ and His Steam Shovel
- 11. Maniac walked barefoot through it
- 12. Maniac taught Grayson to do it
- 14. Age when Jeffrey became an orphan
- 15. Maniac lived there when he knew Grayson: ___ shell
- 16. Maniac and Mars Bar ate dinner with them
- 17. End where the blacks lived
- 19. Uncle __ didn't talk to his wife
- 21. Maniac took one every night with Hester and Lester
- 22. The book Maniac wrote for Grayson: The Man Who Struck Out Willie ___
- 24. Grayson lived there when he met Maniac

Maniac Magee Crossword 2

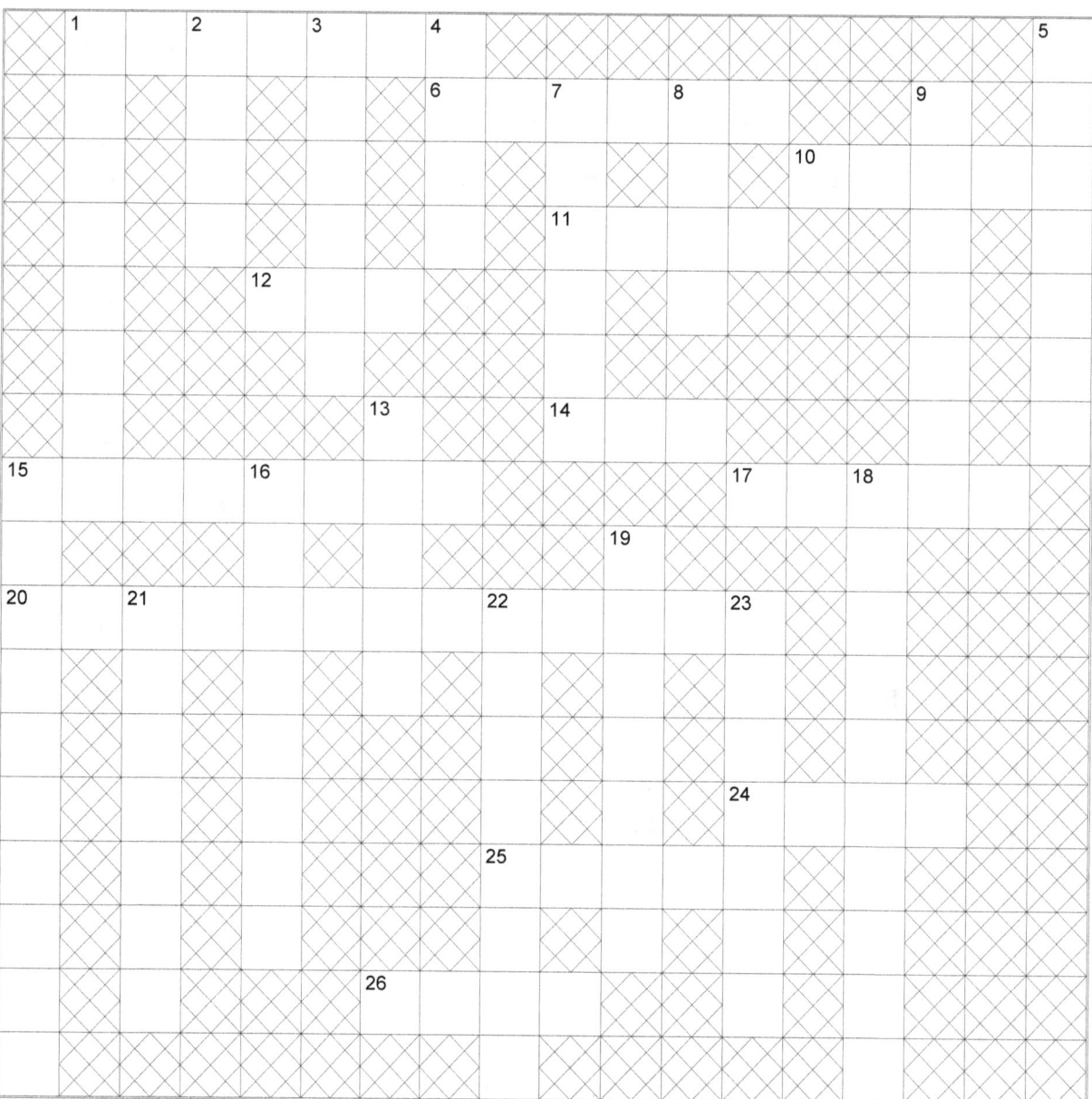

Across
1. Jeffrey kept his room clean
6. She had a suitcase full of books
10. Age when Jeffrey became an orphan
11. Jeffrey was afraid of losing it
12. Jeffrey did this early in the morning, all over town
14. Uncle ___ didn't talk to his wife
15. Amanda said she was changing Mars Bar's name to this
17. Invited Maniac to his birthday party
20. Where Maniac's aunt and uncle lived
24. Grayson lived there when he met Maniac
25. Where Jeffrey ended up: Two ___
26. Went to the McNab house with Maniac: ___ Bar

Down
1. Grayson's favorite book: Mike ___ and His Steam Shovel
2. Maniac taught Grayson to do it
3. McNab's group of friends
4. End where the blacks lived
5. Russell was stuck on it
7. High school kids put him in Finsterwald's yard
8. Maniac walked barefoot through it
9. Title of book Maniac borrowed from Amanda: Children's ___
13. Star quarterback
15. The trolley car fell off the track and into this river
16. Maniac liked to eat butterscotch ones
18. Maniac slept on them: chest ___
19. Maniac kissed a baby one
21. Amanda said Maniac could not get this card without an address
22. The Beale family lived on this street
23. Taught Maniac to play baseball

Maniac Magee Crossword 2 Answer Key

	1 M	2 R	3 A	4 E						5 T
	U	E	O	6 A	7 M	8 N	D	A	9 C	R
	L	A	B	S	R	U	10 T	H	R	E	E
	L	D	R	T	11 N	A	M	E	U	S
	I	12 R	A	N	O	P			S	T
	G		S		L				A	L
	A		13 B	14 D	A	N			D	E
15 S	N	16 I	C	K	E	R	S			17 P	18 P	E	R
C			R		I			19 B		R	
20 H	21 O	L	L	I	D	A	Y	22 S	B	U	23 G	R	O
U		I		M			N	Y		F	R	T
Y		B		P			C		F	A	E
L		R		E			A		A	24 Y	M	C	A
K		A		T			25 M	I	L	L	S	T
I		R		S			O		O	O	O
L		Y		26 M	A	R	S			N	R
L							E				S

Across
1. Jeffrey kept his room clean
6. She had a suitcase full of books
10. Age when Jeffrey became an orphan
11. Jeffrey was afraid of losing it
12. Jeffrey did this early in the morning, all over town
14. Uncle ___ didn't talk to his wife
15. Amanda said she was changing Mars Bar's name to this
17. Invited Maniac to his birthday party
20. Where Maniac's aunt and uncle lived
24. Grayson lived there when he met Maniac
25. Where Jeffrey ended up: Two ___
26. Went to the McNab house with Maniac: ___ Bar

Down
1. Grayson's favorite book: Mike ___ and His Steam Shovel
2. Maniac taught Grayson to do it
3. McNab's group of friends
4. End where the blacks lived
5. Russell was stuck on it
7. High school kids put him in Finsterwald's yard
8. Maniac walked barefoot through it
9. Title of book Maniac borrowed from Amanda: Children's ___
13. Star quarterback
15. The trolley car fell off the track and into this river
16. Maniac liked to eat butterscotch ones
18. Maniac slept on them: chest ___
19. Maniac kissed a baby one
21. Amanda said Maniac could not get this card without an address
22. The Beale family lived on this street
23. Taught Maniac to play baseball

Maniac Magee Crossword 3

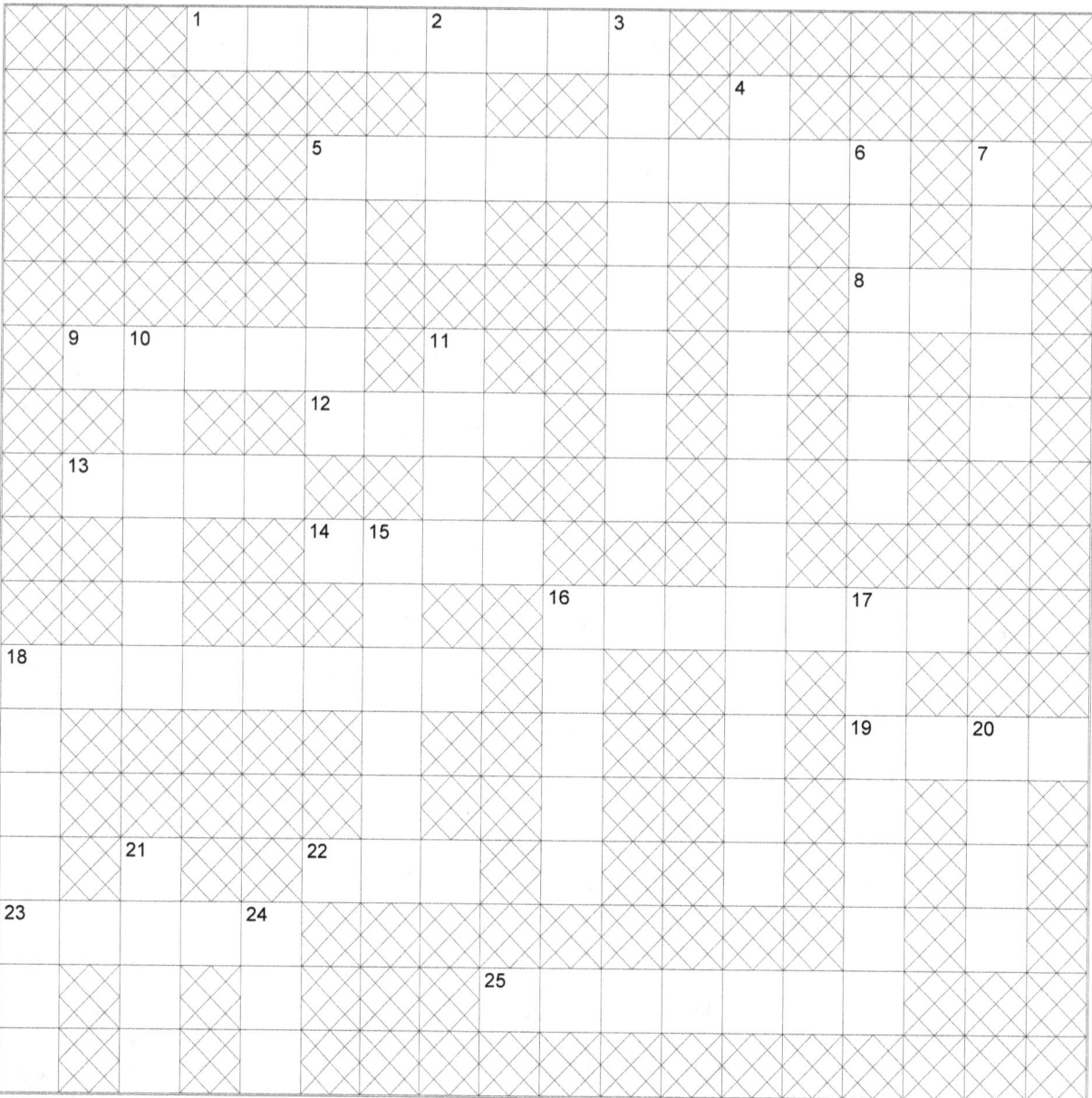

Across
1. Amanda said she was changing Mars Bar's name to this
5. Maniac slept on them: chest ___
8. Jeffrey did this early in the morning, all over town
9. Grayson's Christmas present to Maniac
12. Maniac taught Grayson to do it
13. Largest player in the Little League
14. End where the blacks lived
16. Russell was stuck on it
18. Grayson's favorite book: Mike ___ and His Steam Shovel
19. Maniac lived there when he knew Grayson: ___ shell
22. Uncle __ didn't talk to his wife
23. First book Grayson read: The Little Engine That ___
25. Maniac's real first name

Down
2. Made of string with lots of contortions: cobble's ___
3. The Beale family lived on this street
4. Where Maniac's aunt and uncle lived
5. Invited Maniac to his birthday party
6. Jeffrey did it during the concert
7. Receiver doing a fly pattern: ___ down
10. Jeffrey's middle name
11. Went to the McNab house with Maniac: ___ Bar
15. She had a suitcase full of books
16. Age when Jeffrey became an orphan
17. Amanda said Maniac could not get this card without an address
18. Jeffrey kept his room clean
20. Jeffrey was afraid of losing it
21. Maniac walked barefoot through it
24. Aunt ___ hated her husband

Maniac Magee Crossword 3 Answer Key

		1 S	N	I	2 C	K	E	R	3 S				
					N				Y		4 H		
				5 P	R	O	T	E	C	T	O	R	S	6 S	7 H
				I		T			A		L		C	A
				P					M		L		8 R	A	N
	9 G	10 L	O	V	E		11 M		O		I		E		D
		I			12 R	E	A	D		R		D		A		S
	13 J	O	H	N			R			E		A		M	
		N			14 E	15 A	S	T				Y			
		E				M			16 T	R	E	S	T	17 L	E
18 M	U	L	L	I	G	A	N		H			B		I	
I						N			R			U		19 B	A	20 N	D
R						D			E			R		R		A
A		21 D			22 D	A	N		E			G		A		M
23 C	O	U	L	24 D										R		E
L		M		O				25 J	E	F	F	R	E	Y
E		P		T										

Across
1. Amanda said she was changing Mars Bar's name to this
5. Maniac slept on them: chest ___
8. Jeffrey did this early in the morning, all over town
9. Grayson's Christmas present to Maniac
12. Maniac taught Grayson to do it
13. Largest player in the Little League
14. End where the blacks lived
16. Russell was stuck on it
18. Grayson's favorite book: Mike ___ and His Steam Shovel
19. Maniac lived there when he knew Grayson: ___ shell
22. Uncle __ didn't talk to his wife
23. First book Grayson read: The Little Engine That ___
25. Maniac's real first name

Down
2. Made of string with lots of contortions: cobble's ___
3. The Beale family lived on this street
4. Where Maniac's aunt and uncle lived
5. Invited Maniac to his birthday party
6. Jeffrey did it during the concert
7. Receiver doing a fly pattern: ___ down
10. Jeffrey's middle name
11. Went to the McNab house with Maniac: ___ Bar
15. She had a suitcase full of books
16. Age when Jeffrey became an orphan
17. Amanda said Maniac could not get this card without an address
18. Jeffrey kept his room clean
20. Jeffrey was afraid of losing it
21. Maniac walked barefoot through it
24. Aunt ___ hated her husband

Maniac Magee Crossword 4

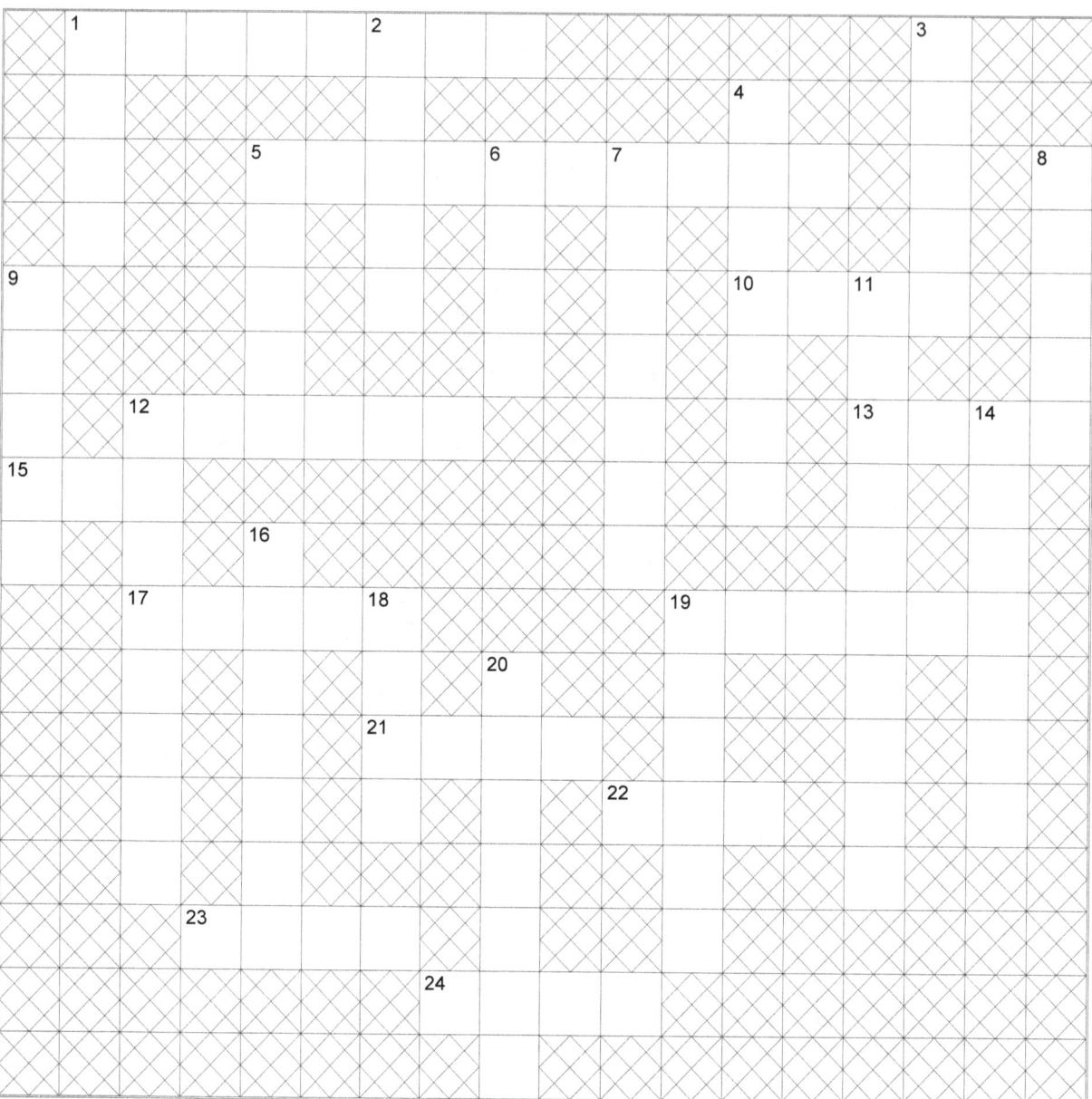

Across
1. Grayson's favorite book: Mike ___ and His Steam Shovel
5. Maniac slept on them: chest ___
10. Grayson lived there when he met Maniac
12. Jeffrey did it during the concert
13. Jeffrey was afraid of losing it
15. Uncle ___ didn't talk to his wife
17. First book Grayson read: The Little Engine That ___
19. She had a suitcase full of books
21. The book Maniac wrote for Grayson: The Man Who Struck Out Willie ___
22. Aunt ___ hated her husband
23. Largest player in the Little League
24. Made of string with lots of contortions: cobble's ___

Down
1. Went to the McNab house with Maniac: ___ Bar
2. Grayson's Christmas present to Maniac
3. Maniac was allergic to it
4. Taught Maniac to play baseball
5. Invited Maniac to his birthday party
6. End where the blacks lived
7. Russell was stuck on it
8. Age when Jeffrey became an orphan
9. Receiver doing a fly pattern: ___ down
11. Easy for Grayson to learn
12. Amanda said she was changing Mars Bar's name to this
14. Jeffrey kept his room clean
16. Maniac kissed a baby one
18. Maniac walked barefoot through it
19. High school kids put him in Finsterwald's yard
20. Kids had a swimming party there: fire ___

Maniac Magee Crossword 4 Answer Key

	1 M	U	L	L	2 I	G	A	N				3 P	
	A				L					4 G		I	
	R		5 P	R	O	T	6 E	7 C	T	O	R	S		Z	8 T
	S		I		V		A		R			A		Z	H
9 H			P		E		S		E		10 Y	M	11 C	A	R
A			E				T		S		S		O		E
N		12 S	C	R	E	A	M		T		O		13 N	14 A	M	E
15 D	A	N							L		N		S	I	
S		I		16 B					E				O	R	
		17 C	O	U	L	D				19 A	M	A	N	D	A
		K		F			20 H			R			A	C	
		E		F		21 M	A	Y	S		N			N	L
		R		A		P			22 D	O	T		T	E
		S		L			R		L			S	
			23 J	O	H	N		A		D		
					24 K	N	O	T			
						T				

Across
1. Grayson's favorite book: Mike ___ and His Steam Shovel
5. Maniac slept on them: chest ___
10. Grayson lived there when he met Maniac
12. Jeffrey did it during the concert
13. Jeffrey was afraid of losing it
15. Uncle __ didn't talk to his wife
17. First book Grayson read: The Little Engine That ___
19. She had a suitcase full of books
21. The book Maniac wrote for Grayson: The Man Who Struck Out Willie ___
22. Aunt ___ hated her husband
23. Largest player in the Little League
24. Made of string with lots of contortions: cobble's ___

Down
1. Went to the McNab house with Maniac: ___ Bar
2. Grayson's Christmas present to Maniac
3. Maniac was allergic to it
4. Taught Maniac to play baseball
5. Invited Maniac to his birthday party
6. End where the blacks lived
7. Russell was stuck on it
8. Age when Jeffrey became an orphan
9. Receiver doing a fly pattern: ___ down
11. Easy for Grayson to learn
12. Amanda said she was changing Mars Bar's name to this
14. Jeffrey kept his room clean
16. Maniac kissed a baby one
18. Maniac walked barefoot through it
19. High school kids put him in Finsterwald's yard
20. Kids had a swimming party there: fire ___

Maniac Magee

COULD	ARNOLD	CONFETTI	EAST	MILLS
SCHUYLKILL	SYCAMORE	GEORGE	COBRAS	PILLBOX
DOT	KRIMPETS	FREE SPACE	GLOVE	ELMWOOD
LIBRARY	PITCHER	RAN	ENCYCLOPEDIA	THREE
PIZZA	FROGBALL	KNOT	VALLEY	DUMP

Maniac Magee

TRASH	MAYS	CONTENT	MARS	BETHANY
HANDS	HYDRANT	BATH	SNICKERS	BRIAN
GRAYSON	LIONEL	FREE SPACE	BAND	AMANDA
BRIDGEPORT	READ	MIRACLE	TRAIN	HOLLIDAYSBURG
THOMPSON	LESTER	PICKWELLS	MINORS	JOHN

Maniac Magee

MAYS	PIZZA	HESTER	KRIMPETS	YMCA
RUSSELL	LIBRARY	MINORS	SYCAMORE	VOWELS
FINSTERWALD	DUMP	FREE SPACE	MILLS	LESTER
JOHN	VALLEY	HANDS	COBRAS	PICKWELLS
BUFFALO	EAST	SCREAM	DOT	THOMPSON

Maniac Magee

COULD	LIONEL	TRAIN	GRAYSON	ARNOLD
MULLIGAN	GEORGE	PITCHER	BAND	POLKAS
JEFFREY	BATH	FREE SPACE	BRIAN	HECTOR
CONTENT	SCHUYLKILL	HYDRANT	ELMWOOD	HOLLIDAYSBURG
PIPER	CONSONANTS	TRASH	TRESTLE	MARS

Maniac Magee

SCREAM	MAYS	MIRACLE	FINSTERWALD	MILLS
GLOVE	HYDRANT	PITCHER	CONTENT	GEORGE
BUFFALO	MINORS	FREE SPACE	NAME	MULLIGAN
SCHUYLKILL	ENCYCLOPEDIA	FROGBALL	CONFETTI	VALLEY
LIBRARY	DUMP	SYCAMORE	READ	CRUSADE

Maniac Magee

BATH	KRIMPETS	ARNOLD	HESTER	LESTER
PILLBOX	ELMWOOD	JOHN	HECTOR	LIONEL
TRESTLE	EAST	FREE SPACE	POLKAS	SNICKERS
BRIAN	KNOT	VOWELS	AMANDA	THOMPSON
HOLLIDAYSBURG	RAN	TRASH	MARS	JEFFREY

Maniac Magee

SCHUYLKILL	HOLLIDAYSBURG	TRASH	HANDS	LIBRARY
PIZZA	FROGBALL	CRUSADE	BRIDGEPORT	HYDRANT
ENCYCLOPEDIA	POLKAS	FREE SPACE	MIRACLE	PIPER
SCREAM	PITCHER	MILLS	THOMPSON	RAN
LIONEL	ARNOLD	CONTENT	RUSSELL	JOHN

Maniac Magee

TRAIN	TRESTLE	DUMP	BAND	BRIAN
PICKWELLS	EAST	BETHANY	MARS	SNICKERS
READ	MINORS	FREE SPACE	JEFFREY	VOWELS
NAME	MAYS	PROTECTORS	SYCAMORE	HESTER
LESTER	KNOT	GRAYSON	DAN	GEORGE

Maniac Magee

RUSSELL	ARNOLD	ENCYCLOPEDIA	RAN	HESTER
JOHN	CRUSADE	ELMWOOD	AMANDA	MARS
BUFFALO	SCHUYLKILL	FREE SPACE	PROTECTORS	TRESTLE
THREE	CONSONANTS	THOMPSON	BATH	LIBRARY
DAN	GRAYSON	CONFETTI	PIZZA	NAME

Maniac Magee

DOT	READ	EAST	LIONEL	COBRAS
MAYS	YMCA	HYDRANT	HECTOR	BAND
FINSTERWALD	BRIDGEPORT	FREE SPACE	COULD	PILLBOX
PICKWELLS	VOWELS	SCREAM	SNICKERS	VALLEY
MULLIGAN	TRASH	GEORGE	MIRACLE	PIPER

Maniac Magee

ELMWOOD	PILLBOX	FINSTERWALD	GEORGE	PITCHER
PROTECTORS	GRAYSON	BAND	SNICKERS	LIBRARY
POLKAS	RUSSELL	FREE SPACE	PIPER	RAN
PIZZA	NAME	GLOVE	THREE	LIONEL
ARNOLD	MULLIGAN	BATH	HYDRANT	FROGBALL

Maniac Magee

DAN	SYCAMORE	DOT	BRIDGEPORT	DUMP
VOWELS	TRAIN	ENCYCLOPEDIA	CRUSADE	JEFFREY
MARS	EAST	FREE SPACE	AMANDA	COULD
BRIAN	HECTOR	HESTER	COBRAS	CONFETTI
JOHN	VALLEY	CONTENT	SCREAM	KNOT

Maniac Magee

SCHUYLKILL	NAME	KRIMPETS	BUFFALO	PIZZA
TRESTLE	MAYS	GEORGE	ENCYCLOPEDIA	ARNOLD
PROTECTORS	VOWELS	FREE SPACE	LIONEL	PIPER
SNICKERS	MIRACLE	BRIAN	HANDS	BRIDGEPORT
READ	THOMPSON	TRASH	ELMWOOD	PITCHER

Maniac Magee

FINSTERWALD	MINORS	PILLBOX	EAST	COULD
DAN	GLOVE	CONTENT	COBRAS	RUSSELL
THREE	PICKWELLS	FREE SPACE	SYCAMORE	LESTER
VALLEY	CONSONANTS	HYDRANT	BATH	HESTER
LIBRARY	DOT	DUMP	KNOT	AMANDA

Maniac Magee

YMCA	BRIDGEPORT	MINORS	PITCHER	GEORGE
PICKWELLS	HECTOR	HOLLIDAYSBURG	CRUSADE	FINSTERWALD
DUMP	RUSSELL	FREE SPACE	BUFFALO	HANDS
CONTENT	MILLS	DAN	FROGBALL	TRASH
BATH	TRESTLE	GRAYSON	CONFETTI	MIRACLE

Maniac Magee

PIZZA	COULD	KRIMPETS	ELMWOOD	MARS
PILLBOX	ARNOLD	GLOVE	VOWELS	LIONEL
BETHANY	KNOT	FREE SPACE	HESTER	SNICKERS
THREE	JOHN	MULLIGAN	COBRAS	POLKAS
SYCAMORE	PIPER	ENCYCLOPEDIA	SCHUYLKILL	TRAIN

Maniac Magee

THOMPSON	PIPER	SYCAMORE	RAN	TRESTLE
DUMP	TRAIN	MULLIGAN	RUSSELL	READ
EAST	LIBRARY	FREE SPACE	FROGBALL	CRUSADE
LESTER	PICKWELLS	BRIDGEPORT	AMANDA	MILLS
PROTECTORS	HESTER	BETHANY	DOT	POLKAS

Maniac Magee

CONSONANTS	LIONEL	ELMWOOD	KRIMPETS	BRIAN
SCHUYLKILL	VALLEY	JEFFREY	PIZZA	BATH
HYDRANT	FINSTERWALD	FREE SPACE	GLOVE	THREE
BAND	COULD	HOLLIDAYSBURG	MARS	GEORGE
CONTENT	ARNOLD	GRAYSON	YMCA	MAYS

Maniac Magee

KNOT	YMCA	BAND	JOHN	SCREAM
DAN	COBRAS	DOT	MAYS	EAST
PIZZA	LIONEL	FREE SPACE	CONTENT	MILLS
MULLIGAN	GEORGE	MINORS	NAME	RUSSELL
BUFFALO	FINSTERWALD	PILLBOX	KRIMPETS	VOWELS

Maniac Magee

HANDS	FROGBALL	PICKWELLS	RAN	THREE
SYCAMORE	THOMPSON	CRUSADE	BETHANY	HECTOR
READ	HYDRANT	FREE SPACE	PROTECTORS	ARNOLD
TRESTLE	GLOVE	CONSONANTS	HOLLIDAYSBURG	PIPER
LIBRARY	JEFFREY	POLKAS	MIRACLE	SNICKERS

Maniac Magee

SYCAMORE	MAYS	SNICKERS	MULLIGAN	DUMP
VOWELS	PIPER	MIRACLE	NAME	ENCYCLOPEDIA
BUFFALO	HOLLIDAYSBURG	FREE SPACE	READ	PIZZA
KNOT	HYDRANT	CONTENT	GRAYSON	ARNOLD
COULD	TRASH	JOHN	BETHANY	HECTOR

Maniac Magee

SCHUYLKILL	LESTER	MARS	PROTECTORS	KRIMPETS
YMCA	GLOVE	GEORGE	PILLBOX	CRUSADE
BAND	LIONEL	FREE SPACE	LIBRARY	FROGBALL
DAN	TRESTLE	AMANDA	TRAIN	HANDS
BRIDGEPORT	RAN	MILLS	EAST	JEFFREY

Maniac Magee

LESTER	COULD	CONSONANTS	MARS	BATH
THOMPSON	CRUSADE	HECTOR	LIONEL	PROTECTORS
GEORGE	COBRAS	FREE SPACE	PITCHER	DAN
BETHANY	FINSTERWALD	GRAYSON	KNOT	TRAIN
MULLIGAN	RAN	BRIDGEPORT	SCHUYLKILL	HYDRANT

Maniac Magee

EAST	PIZZA	BUFFALO	PICKWELLS	JEFFREY
MILLS	POLKAS	MAYS	CONFETTI	KRIMPETS
RUSSELL	READ	FREE SPACE	HOLLIDAYSBURG	BAND
DUMP	DOT	GLOVE	SCREAM	PIPER
NAME	SNICKERS	BRIAN	VALLEY	CONTENT

Maniac Magee

SCHUYLKILL	HANDS	SYCAMORE	MARS	LIONEL
GEORGE	READ	THOMPSON	LIBRARY	CONSONANTS
NAME	TRASH	FREE SPACE	COULD	CRUSADE
DUMP	ELMWOOD	EAST	HYDRANT	BETHANY
SCREAM	MULLIGAN	BRIAN	BAND	YMCA

Maniac Magee

PROTECTORS	GLOVE	DAN	PILLBOX	HOLLIDAYSBURG
PICKWELLS	CONFETTI	MILLS	FROGBALL	VOWELS
HESTER	BRIDGEPORT	FREE SPACE	COBRAS	JEFFREY
VALLEY	ENCYCLOPEDIA	HECTOR	KRIMPETS	BUFFALO
TRAIN	POLKAS	FINSTERWALD	PITCHER	GRAYSON

Maniac Magee

FROGBALL	READ	PROTECTORS	HOLLIDAYSBURG	TRESTLE
MAYS	BRIAN	LIONEL	SCHUYLKILL	KRIMPETS
JOHN	CONSONANTS	FREE SPACE	BRIDGEPORT	BAND
EAST	TRASH	GLOVE	ENCYCLOPEDIA	SNICKERS
YMCA	THOMPSON	ELMWOOD	THREE	LESTER

Maniac Magee

HECTOR	SYCAMORE	BUFFALO	BATH	DOT
CRUSADE	SCREAM	FINSTERWALD	PIZZA	MULLIGAN
ARNOLD	MINORS	FREE SPACE	RUSSELL	KNOT
PITCHER	HYDRANT	AMANDA	COBRAS	GEORGE
RAN	CONTENT	DUMP	JEFFREY	PILLBOX

Maniac Magee

GLOVE	JOHN	HOLLIDAYSBURG	AMANDA	GRAYSON
MARS	PITCHER	TRESTLE	PIZZA	SYCAMORE
NAME	PIPER	FREE SPACE	VOWELS	DUMP
SNICKERS	FINSTERWALD	PICKWELLS	PROTECTORS	RUSSELL
MILLS	COBRAS	YMCA	TRASH	LIONEL

Maniac Magee

GEORGE	HECTOR	LESTER	VALLEY	BRIDGEPORT
BAND	SCREAM	BATH	HYDRANT	MIRACLE
HANDS	MINORS	FREE SPACE	CONTENT	JEFFREY
SCHUYLKILL	BETHANY	THOMPSON	RAN	READ
DOT	EAST	MAYS	TRAIN	CONSONANTS

Maniac Magee

READ	HESTER	MINORS	CONFETTI	THOMPSON
PROTECTORS	TRASH	ENCYCLOPEDIA	SCREAM	SYCAMORE
MIRACLE	JOHN	FREE SPACE	BRIAN	CONSONANTS
GLOVE	PICKWELLS	MILLS	BATH	BRIDGEPORT
ARNOLD	EAST	GEORGE	PIPER	SNICKERS

Maniac Magee

KRIMPETS	AMANDA	POLKAS	THREE	SCHUYLKILL
VALLEY	HECTOR	JEFFREY	DUMP	MAYS
BETHANY	GRAYSON	FREE SPACE	FROGBALL	MARS
ELMWOOD	DOT	PIZZA	VOWELS	LESTER
COBRAS	DAN	MULLIGAN	NAME	CONTENT

Maniac Magee Vocabulary Word List

No.	Word	Clue/Definition
1.	ACCURATE	Exactly correct
2.	APPARENTLY	Easily understood
3.	BELLOWING	Yelling
4.	BLUNDERING	Moving in a clumsy way
5.	CHAOTIC	Disorderly
6.	CLENCHED	Grasped tightly
7.	COMMOTION	Disturbance
8.	COMPLIMENTS	Acts of courtesy
9.	CONCLUSIONS	End results
10.	CONFINED	Limited
11.	CONTORTIONS	Twisting and bending out of shape
12.	CONVERGED	Came together
13.	CRAMMED	Crowded; packed
14.	CRINGED	Winced; recoiled
15.	CUNNING	Having skill in deception
16.	DANGLED	Hung loosely
17.	DESOLATION	Gloom; bleakness
18.	DIGITS	Number symbols
19.	DUMBFOUNDED	Amazed; astonished
20.	ECSTATIC	Overjoyed
21.	ENDURE	To bear with tolerance
22.	ESCORT	A guide or guard
23.	EXHAUSTION	Complete weariness
24.	EXPIRED	Ended
25.	EXTORT	To get by threats
26.	EXUBERANCE	Enthusiasm
27.	FATAL	Deadly
28.	FINICKY	Choosy; fussy
29.	FLINCHED	Shrank back in fear
30.	FORESIGHT	Looking into the future
31.	GAUNTLET	An attack from all sides
32.	GRATES	Parallel bars for blocking an opening
33.	GRIZZLED	Streaked with gray
34.	GROUSE	Complain; grumble
35.	HALTED	Stopped
36.	HOISTED	Lifted
37.	ILLUSION	Fantasy; false belief
38.	INCUBATING	Developing and hatching
39.	INFAMOUS	Having a very bad reputation
40.	INSTINCTS	Natural impulses or motivations
41.	LANGUISHED	Weakened; faded
42.	LUDICROUS	Ridiculous
43.	LUNGING	Moving forward suddenly
44.	LURCHING	Rolling or pitching suddenly
45.	MAMMOTH	Gigantic; enormous
46.	MANIAC	A person who has extra enthusiasm or desire
47.	MINUTELY	Concerned with small details
48.	OBVIOUS	Apparent; observable
49.	OPPONENT	One against another
50.	PANDEMONIUM	Uproar; confusion
51.	PERILOUS	Dangerous
52.	PREPOSTEROUS	Farfetched
53.	PROMPT	Instant; immediate

Maniac Magee Vocabulary Word List

No.	Word	Clue/Definition
54.	PRONE	Flat
55.	PRY	To force open or up
56.	PURSUERS	Followers trying to overtake; chasers
57.	QUIVER	To shake with a slight movement
58.	RANDOM	Having no pattern or purpose
59.	RANTING	Speaking in a violent manner
60.	RELUCTANT	Unwilling
61.	REPRISALS	Revenge
62.	REVEAL	Make known
63.	RICKETY	Shaky
64.	ROOKIE	A first year player
65.	SCANNED	Looked over quickly
66.	SCOFFING	Jeering
67.	SCOWLING	Wrinkling the forehead in anger
68.	SEETHING	Violently excited
69.	SLEAZY	Shabby and dirty
70.	SOLITUDE	Aloneness
71.	STABILITY	Dependability
72.	STOIC	Indifferent to pain or pleasure
73.	STUNNED	Shocked
74.	SURGED	Moved like waves
75.	VACANT	Empty
76.	VAGUE	Unspecified; unclear
77.	VENTURED	Went in spite of risk
78.	WRENCHED	Twisted
79.	WRETCH	A miserable, unfortunate person

Maniac Magee Vocabulary Fill In The Blank 1

_____ 1. Deadly

_____ 2. To get by threats

_____ 3. Revenge

_____ 4. Shrank back in fear

_____ 5. Number symbols

_____ 6. Shabby and dirty

_____ 7. Indifferent to pain or pleasure

_____ 8. Gigantic; enormous

_____ 9. Having no pattern or purpose

_____ 10. Ended

_____ 11. Dangerous

_____ 12. Rolling or pitching suddenly

_____ 13. Concerned with small details

_____ 14. Went in spite of risk

_____ 15. A person who has extra enthusiasm or desire

_____ 16. Natural impulses or motivations

_____ 17. To bear with tolerance

_____ 18. A first year player

_____ 19. Shaky

_____ 20. Weakened; faded

Maniac Magee Vocabulary Fill In The Blank 1 Answer Key

FATAL	1. Deadly
EXTORT	2. To get by threats
REPRISALS	3. Revenge
FLINCHED	4. Shrank back in fear
DIGITS	5. Number symbols
SLEAZY	6. Shabby and dirty
STOIC	7. Indifferent to pain or pleasure
MAMMOTH	8. Gigantic; enormous
RANDOM	9. Having no pattern or purpose
EXPIRED	10. Ended
PERILOUS	11. Dangerous
LURCHING	12. Rolling or pitching suddenly
MINUTELY	13. Concerned with small details
VENTURED	14. Went in spite of risk
MANIAC	15. A person who has extra enthusiasm or desire
INSTINCTS	16. Natural impulses or motivations
ENDURE	17. To bear with tolerance
ROOKIE	18. A first year player
RICKETY	19. Shaky
LANGUISHED	20. Weakened; faded

Maniac Magee Vocabulary Fill In The Blank 2

_____ 1. Choosy; fussy

_____ 2. A miserable, unfortunate person

_____ 3. Hung loosely

_____ 4. Overjoyed

_____ 5. Ended

_____ 6. Gigantic; enormous

_____ 7. Rolling or pitching suddenly

_____ 8. Instant; immediate

_____ 9. Yelling

_____ 10. Apparent; observable

_____ 11. Unspecified; unclear

_____ 12. Shocked

_____ 13. Shabby and dirty

_____ 14. Having skill in deception

_____ 15. Amazed; astonished

_____ 16. To bear with tolerance

_____ 17. Violently excited

_____ 18. Wrinkling the forehead in anger

_____ 19. A guide or guard

_____ 20. Having a very bad reputation

Maniac Magee Vocabulary Fill In The Blank 2 Answer Key

FINICKY	1. Choosy; fussy
WRETCH	2. A miserable, unfortunate person
DANGLED	3. Hung loosely
ECSTATIC	4. Overjoyed
EXPIRED	5. Ended
MAMMOTH	6. Gigantic; enormous
LURCHING	7. Rolling or pitching suddenly
PROMPT	8. Instant; immediate
BELLOWING	9. Yelling
OBVIOUS	10. Apparent; observable
VAGUE	11. Unspecified; unclear
STUNNED	12. Shocked
SLEAZY	13. Shabby and dirty
CUNNING	14. Having skill in deception
DUMBFOUNDED	15. Amazed; astonished
ENDURE	16. To bear with tolerance
SEETHING	17. Violently excited
SCOWLING	18. Wrinkling the forehead in anger
ESCORT	19. A guide or guard
INFAMOUS	20. Having a very bad reputation

Maniac Magee Vocabulary Fill In The Blank 3

_____ 1. To get by threats
_____ 2. Wrinkling the forehead in anger
_____ 3. Limited
_____ 4. Enthusiasm
_____ 5. Followers trying to overtake; chasers
_____ 6. Speaking in a violent manner
_____ 7. Fantasy; false belief
_____ 8. Having skill in deception
_____ 9. A person who has extra enthusiasm or desire
_____ 10. Number symbols
_____ 11. End results
_____ 12. A guide or guard
_____ 13. One against another
_____ 14. Deadly
_____ 15. Hung loosely
_____ 16. Shaky
_____ 17. Looked over quickly
_____ 18. Exactly correct
_____ 19. Twisted
_____ 20. To shake with a slight movement

Maniac Magee Vocabulary Fill In The Blank 3 Answer Key

EXTORT	1. To get by threats
SCOWLING	2. Wrinkling the forehead in anger
CONFINED	3. Limited
EXUBERANCE	4. Enthusiasm
PURSUERS	5. Followers trying to overtake; chasers
RANTING	6. Speaking in a violent manner
ILLUSION	7. Fantasy; false belief
CUNNING	8. Having skill in deception
MANIAC	9. A person who has extra enthusiasm or desire
DIGITS	10. Number symbols
CONCLUSIONS	11. End results
ESCORT	12. A guide or guard
OPPONENT	13. One against another
FATAL	14. Deadly
DANGLED	15. Hung loosely
RICKETY	16. Shaky
SCANNED	17. Looked over quickly
ACCURATE	18. Exactly correct
WRENCHED	19. Twisted
QUIVER	20. To shake with a slight movement

Maniac Magee Vocabulary Fill In The Blank 4

_____ 1. Gloom; bleakness
_____ 2. Having skill in deception
_____ 3. Jeering
_____ 4. Instant; immediate
_____ 5. Overjoyed
_____ 6. Disturbance
_____ 7. Looking into the future
_____ 8. Ended
_____ 9. Twisted
_____ 10. Empty
_____ 11. Went in spite of risk
_____ 12. Followers trying to overtake; chasers
_____ 13. To force open or up
_____ 14. Exactly correct
_____ 15. Amazed; astonished
_____ 16. Moved like waves
_____ 17. Farfetched
_____ 18. Uproar; confusion
_____ 19. Rolling or pitching suddenly
_____ 20. Speaking in a violent manner

Maniac Magee Vocabulary Fill In The Blank 4 Answer Key

DESOLATION	1. Gloom; bleakness
CUNNING	2. Having skill in deception
SCOFFING	3. Jeering
PROMPT	4. Instant; immediate
ECSTATIC	5. Overjoyed
COMMOTION	6. Disturbance
FORESIGHT	7. Looking into the future
EXPIRED	8. Ended
WRENCHED	9. Twisted
VACANT	10. Empty
VENTURED	11. Went in spite of risk
PURSUERS	12. Followers trying to overtake; chasers
PRY	13. To force open or up
ACCURATE	14. Exactly correct
DUMBFOUNDED	15. Amazed; astonished
SURGED	16. Moved like waves
PREPOSTEROUS	17. Farfetched
PANDEMONIUM	18. Uproar; confusion
LURCHING	19. Rolling or pitching suddenly
RANTING	20. Speaking in a violent manner

Maniac Magee Vocabulary Matching 1

___ 1. SLEAZY   A. A first year player
___ 2. OPPONENT   B. An attack from all sides
___ 3. ROOKIE   C. Revenge
___ 4. STUNNED   D. Hung loosely
___ 5. RICKETY   E. Dangerous
___ 6. CRAMMED   F. Violently excited
___ 7. RELUCTANT   G. Shocked
___ 8. EXUBERANCE   H. Enthusiasm
___ 9. MAMMOTH   I. Having no pattern or purpose
___ 10. GAUNTLET   J. A miserable, unfortunate person
___ 11. RANDOM   K. Aloneness
___ 12. SEETHING   L. Gigantic; enormous
___ 13. FATAL   M. Moving in a clumsy way
___ 14. BLUNDERING   N. Complete weariness
___ 15. WRETCH   O. Deadly
___ 16. SOLITUDE   P. Unwilling
___ 17. LURCHING   Q. Twisted
___ 18. CONTORTIONS   R. Shabby and dirty
___ 19. EXHAUSTION   S. Shaky
___ 20. ACCURATE   T. Gloom; bleakness
___ 21. WRENCHED   U. Crowded; packed
___ 22. REPRISALS   V. One against another
___ 23. PERILOUS   W. Twisting and bending out of shape
___ 24. DESOLATION   X. Exactly correct
___ 25. DANGLED   Y. Rolling or pitching suddenly

Maniac Magee Vocabulary Matching 1 Answer Key

R - 1.	SLEAZY	A.	A first year player
V - 2.	OPPONENT	B.	An attack from all sides
A - 3.	ROOKIE	C.	Revenge
G - 4.	STUNNED	D.	Hung loosely
S - 5.	RICKETY	E.	Dangerous
U - 6.	CRAMMED	F.	Violently excited
P - 7.	RELUCTANT	G.	Shocked
H - 8.	EXUBERANCE	H.	Enthusiasm
L - 9.	MAMMOTH	I.	Having no pattern or purpose
B - 10.	GAUNTLET	J.	A miserable, unfortunate person
I - 11.	RANDOM	K.	Aloneness
F - 12.	SEETHING	L.	Gigantic; enormous
O - 13.	FATAL	M.	Moving in a clumsy way
M - 14.	BLUNDERING	N.	Complete weariness
J - 15.	WRETCH	O.	Deadly
K - 16.	SOLITUDE	P.	Unwilling
Y - 17.	LURCHING	Q.	Twisted
W - 18.	CONTORTIONS	R.	Shabby and dirty
N - 19.	EXHAUSTION	S.	Shaky
X - 20.	ACCURATE	T.	Gloom; bleakness
Q - 21.	WRENCHED	U.	Crowded; packed
C - 22.	REPRISALS	V.	One against another
E - 23.	PERILOUS	W.	Twisting and bending out of shape
T - 24.	DESOLATION	X.	Exactly correct
D - 25.	DANGLED	Y.	Rolling or pitching suddenly

Maniac Magee Vocabulary Matching 2

___ 1. WRETCH   A. To bear with tolerance
___ 2. ENDURE   B. Having a very bad reputation
___ 3. VACANT   C. Empty
___ 4. MAMMOTH   D. Easily understood
___ 5. CONTORTIONS   E. One against another
___ 6. CONCLUSIONS   F. Moving forward suddenly
___ 7. CRAMMED   G. Twisting and bending out of shape
___ 8. FINICKY   H. Flat
___ 9. MINUTELY   I. Came together
___ 10. LANGUISHED   J. A miserable, unfortunate person
___ 11. PREPOSTEROUS   K. A person who has extra enthusiasm or desire
___ 12. APPARENTLY   L. Revenge
___ 13. LUNGING   M. Concerned with small details
___ 14. RANTING   N. Overjoyed
___ 15. OPPONENT   O. Gigantic; enormous
___ 16. CHAOTIC   P. Disorderly
___ 17. ROOKIE   Q. End results
___ 18. CONVERGED   R. Gloom; bleakness
___ 19. REPRISALS   S. A first year player
___ 20. RICKETY   T. Speaking in a violent manner
___ 21. MANIAC   U. Farfetched
___ 22. ECSTATIC   V. Weakened; faded
___ 23. DESOLATION   W. Shaky
___ 24. PRONE   X. Crowded; packed
___ 25. INFAMOUS   Y. Choosy; fussy

Maniac Magee Vocabulary Matching 2 Answer Key

J - 1.	WRETCH	A.	To bear with tolerance
A - 2.	ENDURE	B.	Having a very bad reputation
C - 3.	VACANT	C.	Empty
O - 4.	MAMMOTH	D.	Easily understood
G - 5.	CONTORTIONS	E.	One against another
Q - 6.	CONCLUSIONS	F.	Moving forward suddenly
X - 7.	CRAMMED	G.	Twisting and bending out of shape
Y - 8.	FINICKY	H.	Flat
M - 9.	MINUTELY	I.	Came together
V - 10.	LANGUISHED	J.	A miserable, unfortunate person
U - 11.	PREPOSTEROUS	K.	A person who has extra enthusiasm or desire
D - 12.	APPARENTLY	L.	Revenge
F - 13.	LUNGING	M.	Concerned with small details
T - 14.	RANTING	N.	Overjoyed
E - 15.	OPPONENT	O.	Gigantic; enormous
P - 16.	CHAOTIC	P.	Disorderly
S - 17.	ROOKIE	Q.	End results
I - 18.	CONVERGED	R.	Gloom; bleakness
L - 19.	REPRISALS	S.	A first year player
W - 20.	RICKETY	T.	Speaking in a violent manner
K - 21.	MANIAC	U.	Farfetched
N - 22.	ECSTATIC	V.	Weakened; faded
R - 23.	DESOLATION	W.	Shaky
H - 24.	PRONE	X.	Crowded; packed
B - 25.	INFAMOUS	Y.	Choosy; fussy

Maniac Magee Vocabulary Matching 3

___ 1. ENDURE   A. Acts of courtesy

___ 2. MANIAC   B. Twisted

___ 3. CONVERGED   C. Unspecified; unclear

___ 4. COMPLIMENTS   D. Dangerous

___ 5. SOLITUDE   E. To shake with a slight movement

___ 6. PURSUERS   F. Developing and hatching

___ 7. VAGUE   G. Concerned with small details

___ 8. WRENCHED   H. Rolling or pitching suddenly

___ 9. HOISTED   I. To bear with tolerance

___ 10. CUNNING   J. Shaky

___ 11. INCUBATING   K. An attack from all sides

___ 12. FORESIGHT   L. Streaked with gray

___ 13. PERILOUS   M. Looking into the future

___ 14. ESCORT   N. Lifted

___ 15. PREPOSTEROUS   O. Aloneness

___ 16. LURCHING   P. Farfetched

___ 17. HALTED   Q. Shabby and dirty

___ 18. PRONE   R. Followers trying to overtake; chasers

___ 19. SLEAZY   S. A person who has extra enthusiasm or desire

___ 20. MINUTELY   T. A guide or guard

___ 21. FINICKY   U. Having skill in deception

___ 22. RICKETY   V. Stopped

___ 23. QUIVER   W. Flat

___ 24. GRIZZLED   X. Came together

___ 25. GAUNTLET   Y. Choosy; fussy

Maniac Magee Vocabulary Matching 3 Answer Key

I - 1.	ENDURE	A. Acts of courtesy
S - 2.	MANIAC	B. Twisted
X - 3.	CONVERGED	C. Unspecified; unclear
A - 4.	COMPLIMENTS	D. Dangerous
O - 5.	SOLITUDE	E. To shake with a slight movement
R - 6.	PURSUERS	F. Developing and hatching
C - 7.	VAGUE	G. Concerned with small details
B - 8.	WRENCHED	H. Rolling or pitching suddenly
N - 9.	HOISTED	I. To bear with tolerance
U - 10.	CUNNING	J. Shaky
F - 11.	INCUBATING	K. An attack from all sides
M - 12.	FORESIGHT	L. Streaked with gray
D - 13.	PERILOUS	M. Looking into the future
T - 14.	ESCORT	N. Lifted
P - 15.	PREPOSTEROUS	O. Aloneness
H - 16.	LURCHING	P. Farfetched
V - 17.	HALTED	Q. Shabby and dirty
W - 18.	PRONE	R. Followers trying to overtake; chasers
Q - 19.	SLEAZY	S. A person who has extra enthusiasm or desire
G - 20.	MINUTELY	T. A guide or guard
Y - 21.	FINICKY	U. Having skill in deception
J - 22.	RICKETY	V. Stopped
E - 23.	QUIVER	W. Flat
L - 24.	GRIZZLED	X. Came together
K - 25.	GAUNTLET	Y. Choosy; fussy

Maniac Magee Vocabulary Matching 4

___ 1. BELLOWING   A. Moved like waves
___ 2. FLINCHED   B. Empty
___ 3. FINICKY   C. Winced; recoiled
___ 4. PANDEMONIUM   D. Crowded; packed
___ 5. REPRISALS   E. Hung loosely
___ 6. PROMPT   F. Parallel bars for blocking an opening
___ 7. MINUTELY   G. Instant; immediate
___ 8. DANGLED   H. Limited
___ 9. CRAMMED   I. Concerned with small details
___ 10. CONFINED   J. Unwilling
___ 11. PURSUERS   K. A miserable, unfortunate person
___ 12. LANGUISHED   L. Followers trying to overtake; chasers
___ 13. ROOKIE   M. Yelling
___ 14. RELUCTANT   N. To bear with tolerance
___ 15. GRATES   O. End results
___ 16. VACANT   P. Amazed; astonished
___ 17. CRINGED   Q. Indifferent to pain or pleasure
___ 18. ENDURE   R. Overjoyed
___ 19. STOIC   S. Revenge
___ 20. WRETCH   T. Uproar; confusion
___ 21. HOISTED   U. Choosy; fussy
___ 22. ECSTATIC   V. Weakened; faded
___ 23. DUMBFOUNDED   W. Shrank back in fear
___ 24. CONCLUSIONS   X. A first year player
___ 25. SURGED   Y. Lifted

Maniac Magee Vocabulary Matching 4 Answer Key

M - 1. BELLOWING   A. Moved like waves
W - 2. FLINCHED   B. Empty
U - 3. FINICKY   C. Winced; recoiled
T - 4. PANDEMONIUM   D. Crowded; packed
S - 5. REPRISALS   E. Hung loosely
G - 6. PROMPT   F. Parallel bars for blocking an opening
I - 7. MINUTELY   G. Instant; immediate
E - 8. DANGLED   H. Limited
D - 9. CRAMMED   I. Concerned with small details
H - 10. CONFINED   J. Unwilling
L - 11. PURSUERS   K. A miserable, unfortunate person
V - 12. LANGUISHED   L. Followers trying to overtake; chasers
X - 13. ROOKIE   M. Yelling
J - 14. RELUCTANT   N. To bear with tolerance
F - 15. GRATES   O. End results
B - 16. VACANT   P. Amazed; astonished
C - 17. CRINGED   Q. Indifferent to pain or pleasure
N - 18. ENDURE   R. Overjoyed
Q - 19. STOIC   S. Revenge
K - 20. WRETCH   T. Uproar; confusion
Y - 21. HOISTED   U. Choosy; fussy
R - 22. ECSTATIC   V. Weakened; faded
P - 23. DUMBFOUNDED   W. Shrank back in fear
O - 24. CONCLUSIONS   X. A first year player
A - 25. SURGED   Y. Lifted

Maniac Magee Vocabulary Magic Squares 1

Match the definition with the vocabulary word. Put your answers in the magic squares below. When your answers are correct, all columns and rows will add to the same number.

A. CUNNING
B. CONVERGED
C. EXHAUSTION
D. ENDURE
E. ACCURATE
F. GRIZZLED
G. STOIC
H. STUNNED
I. PRONE
J. INCUBATING
K. OPPONENT
L. SCOFFING
M. WRETCH
N. MINUTELY
O. SCOWLING
P. DANGLED

1. Came together
2. Indifferent to pain or pleasure
3. One against another
4. Concerned with small details
5. A miserable, unfortunate person
6. Jeering
7. Shocked
8. Having skill in deception
9. Hung loosely
10. Flat
11. Exactly correct
12. To bear with tolerance
13. Complete weariness
14. Streaked with gray
15. Developing and hatching
16. Wrinkling the forehead in anger

A=	B=	C=	D=
E=	F=	G=	H=
I=	J=	K=	L=
M=	N=	O=	P=

Maniac Magee Vocabulary Magic Squares 1 Answer Key

Match the definition with the vocabulary word. Put your answers in the magic squares below. When your answers are correct, all columns and rows will add to the same number.

A. CUNNING
B. CONVERGED
C. EXHAUSTION
D. ENDURE
E. ACCURATE
F. GRIZZLED
G. STOIC
H. STUNNED
I. PRONE
J. INCUBATING
K. OPPONENT
L. SCOFFING
M. WRETCH
N. MINUTELY
O. SCOWLING
P. DANGLED

1. Came together
2. Indifferent to pain or pleasure
3. One against another
4. Concerned with small details
5. A miserable, unfortunate person
6. Jeering
7. Shocked
8. Having skill in deception
9. Hung loosely
10. Flat
11. Exactly correct
12. To bear with tolerance
13. Complete weariness
14. Streaked with gray
15. Developing and hatching
16. Wrinkling the forehead in anger

A=8	B=1	C=13	D=12
E=11	F=14	G=2	H=7
I=10	J=15	K=3	L=6
M=5	N=4	O=16	P=9

Maniac Magee Vocabulary Magic Squares 2

Match the definition with the vocabulary word. Put your answers in the magic squares below. When your answers are correct, all columns and rows will add to the same number.

A. LUDICROUS
B. SCOWLING
C. ACCURATE
D. CHAOTIC
E. OPPONENT
F. ESCORT
G. GRIZZLED
H. SCANNED
I. PANDEMONIUM
J. RANDOM
K. APPARENTLY
L. DESOLATION
M. INSTINCTS
N. WRENCHED
O. VACANT
P. PERILOUS

1. Exactly correct
2. Having no pattern or purpose
3. A guide or guard
4. Empty
5. Dangerous
6. One against another
7. Uproar; confusion
8. Disorderly
9. Natural impulses or motivations
10. Looked over quickly
11. Gloom; bleakness
12. Ridiculous
13. Wrinkling the forehead in anger
14. Easily understood
15. Streaked with gray
16. Twisted

A=	B=	C=	D=
E=	F=	G=	H=
I=	J=	K=	L=
M=	N=	O=	P=

Maniac Magee Vocabulary Magic Squares 2 Answer Key

Match the definition with the vocabulary word. Put your answers in the magic squares below. When your answers are correct, all columns and rows will add to the same number.

A. LUDICROUS
B. SCOWLING
C. ACCURATE
D. CHAOTIC
E. OPPONENT
F. ESCORT
G. GRIZZLED
H. SCANNED
I. PANDEMONIUM
J. RANDOM
K. APPARENTLY
L. DESOLATION
M. INSTINCTS
N. WRENCHED
O. VACANT
P. PERILOUS

1. Exactly correct
2. Having no pattern or purpose
3. A guide or guard
4. Empty
5. Dangerous
6. One against another
7. Uproar; confusion
8. Disorderly
9. Natural impulses or motivations
10. Looked over quickly
11. Gloom; bleakness
12. Ridiculous
13. Wrinkling the forehead in anger
14. Easily understood
15. Streaked with gray
16. Twisted

A=12	B=13	C=1	D=8
E=6	F=3	G=15	H=10
I=7	J=2	K=14	L=11
M=9	N=16	O=4	P=5

Maniac Magee Vocabulary Magic Squares 3

Match the definition with the vocabulary word. Put your answers in the magic squares below. When your answers are correct, all columns and rows will add to the same number.

A. GROUSE
B. INCUBATING
C. PRY
D. EXTORT
E. ECSTATIC
F. FINICKY
G. EXHAUSTION
H. BLUNDERING
I. GRATES
J. ACCURATE
K. COMMOTION
L. PRONE
M. CUNNING
N. CONFINED
O. CONTORTIONS
P. HALTED

1. Twisting and bending out of shape
2. Exactly correct
3. Moving in a clumsy way
4. Complain; grumble
5. To get by threats
6. Overjoyed
7. Disturbance
8. Limited
9. Choosy; fussy
10. To force open or up
11. Having skill in deception
12. Flat
13. Parallel bars for blocking an opening
14. Stopped
15. Developing and hatching
16. Complete weariness

A=	B=	C=	D=
E=	F=	G=	H=
I=	J=	K=	L=
M=	N=	O=	P=

Maniac Magee Vocabulary Magic Squares 3 Answer Key

Match the definition with the vocabulary word. Put your answers in the magic squares below. When your answers are correct, all columns and rows will add to the same number.

A. GROUSE
B. INCUBATING
C. PRY
D. EXTORT
E. ECSTATIC
F. FINICKY
G. EXHAUSTION
H. BLUNDERING
I. GRATES
J. ACCURATE
K. COMMOTION
L. PRONE
M. CUNNING
N. CONFINED
O. CONTORTIONS
P. HALTED

1. Twisting and bending out of shape
2. Exactly correct
3. Moving in a clumsy way
4. Complain; grumble
5. To get by threats
6. Overjoyed
7. Disturbance
8. Limited
9. Choosy; fussy
10. To force open or up
11. Having skill in deception
12. Flat
13. Parallel bars for blocking an opening
14. Stopped
15. Developing and hatching
16. Complete weariness

A=4	B=15	C=10	D=5
E=6	F=9	G=16	H=3
I=13	J=2	K=7	L=12
M=11	N=8	O=1	P=14

85
Copyrighted

Maniac Magee Vocabulary Magic Squares 4

Match the definition with the vocabulary word. Put your answers in the magic squares below. When your answers are correct, all columns and rows will add to the same number.

A. SCANNED
B. VAGUE
C. VACANT
D. CUNNING
E. SCOFFING
F. CHAOTIC
G. SURGED
H. RANDOM
I. PREPOSTEROUS
J. RELUCTANT
K. EXHAUSTION
L. APPARENTLY
M. BELLOWING
N. FLINCHED
O. BLUNDERING
P. CONCLUSIONS

1. Yelling
2. Disorderly
3. Having no pattern or purpose
4. Moving in a clumsy way
5. Easily understood
6. Empty
7. Looked over quickly
8. Unwilling
9. Complete weariness
10. Having skill in deception
11. Unspecified; unclear
12. Farfetched
13. Shrank back in fear
14. Jeering
15. Moved like waves
16. End results

A=	B=	C=	D=
E=	F=	G=	H=
I=	J=	K=	L=
M=	N=	O=	P=

Maniac Magee Vocabulary Magic Squares 4 Answer Key

Match the definition with the vocabulary word. Put your answers in the magic squares below. When your answers are correct, all columns and rows will add to the same number.

A. SCANNED
B. VAGUE
C. VACANT
D. CUNNING
E. SCOFFING
F. CHAOTIC
G. SURGED
H. RANDOM
I. PREPOSTEROUS
J. RELUCTANT
K. EXHAUSTION
L. APPARENTLY
M. BELLOWING
N. FLINCHED
O. BLUNDERING
P. CONCLUSIONS

1. Yelling
2. Disorderly
3. Having no pattern or purpose
4. Moving in a clumsy way
5. Easily understood
6. Empty
7. Looked over quickly
8. Unwilling
9. Complete weariness
10. Having skill in deception
11. Unspecified; unclear
12. Farfetched
13. Shrank back in fear
14. Jeering
15. Moved like waves
16. End results

A=7	B=11	C=6	D=10
E=14	F=2	G=15	H=3
I=12	J=8	K=9	L=5
M=1	N=13	O=4	P=16

Maniac Magee Vocabulary Word Search 1

```
R E L U C T A N T S G R A N D O M V A T
O D E R I P X E E N R A B F H D U A C P
O A S T S H F T I L O S U D X C I G C V
K N C F A T A L B D U P N G Y N U U G
I G O V V R W L E M S N J R T M O E R F
E L R L G O H M T D E C G E G L M F A Z
F E T R C Y M M E E O N K I Y E E C T H
S D H S R A Q T H N D C S Z N D D T E N
T M M P R T S C T E I U F D T G N L C X
C A N C Y I T O C R O F U R V E A G O R
N N G G O E R N T R S R T T D E P V N M
I I N H R T A F C C E R P U V P Y A F S
T A I W I R K I O O O L T E R P C C I C
S C N O E J D F P T M I R O H R I A N Y
N T N B D U F R X S L M M T G O O N E P
I S U O L I R E P O P P O N E T T D C
V X C N N R G V S M T M Z T M E S Y V Y
E F Q G N L C I C S M T H G I S E R O F
S C A N N E D U T A D S C H A O T I C B
S L E A Z Y D Q M S Q N P C R I N G E D
```

A first year player (6)
A guide or guard (6)
A miserable, unfortunate person (6)
A person who has extra enthusiasm or desire (6)
Aloneness (8)
An attack from all sides (8)
Complain; grumble (6)
Crowded; packed (7)
Dangerous (8)
Deadly (5)
Disorderly (7)
Disturbance (9)
Empty (6)
Ended (7)
Enthusiasm (10)
Exactly correct (8)
Flat (5)
Gigantic; enormous (7)
Having no pattern or purpose (6)
Having skill in deception (7)
Hung loosely (7)
Indifferent to pain or pleasure (5)
Instant; immediate (6)
Jeering (8)
Lifted (7)

Limited (8)
Looked over quickly (7)
Looking into the future (9)
Make known (6)
Moved like waves (6)
Moving forward suddenly (7)
Natural impulses or motivations (9)
Number symbols (6)
One against another (8)
Parallel bars for blocking an opening (6)
Ridiculous (9)
Shabby and dirty (6)
Shaky (7)
Shocked (7)
Stopped (6)
To bear with tolerance (6)
To force open or up (3)
To get by threats (6)
To shake with a slight movement (6)
Twisting and bending out of shape (11)
Unspecified; unclear (5)
Unwilling (9)
Uproar; confusion (11)
Winced; recoiled (7)
Wrinkling the forehead in anger (8)

Maniac Magee Vocabulary Word Search 1 Answer Key

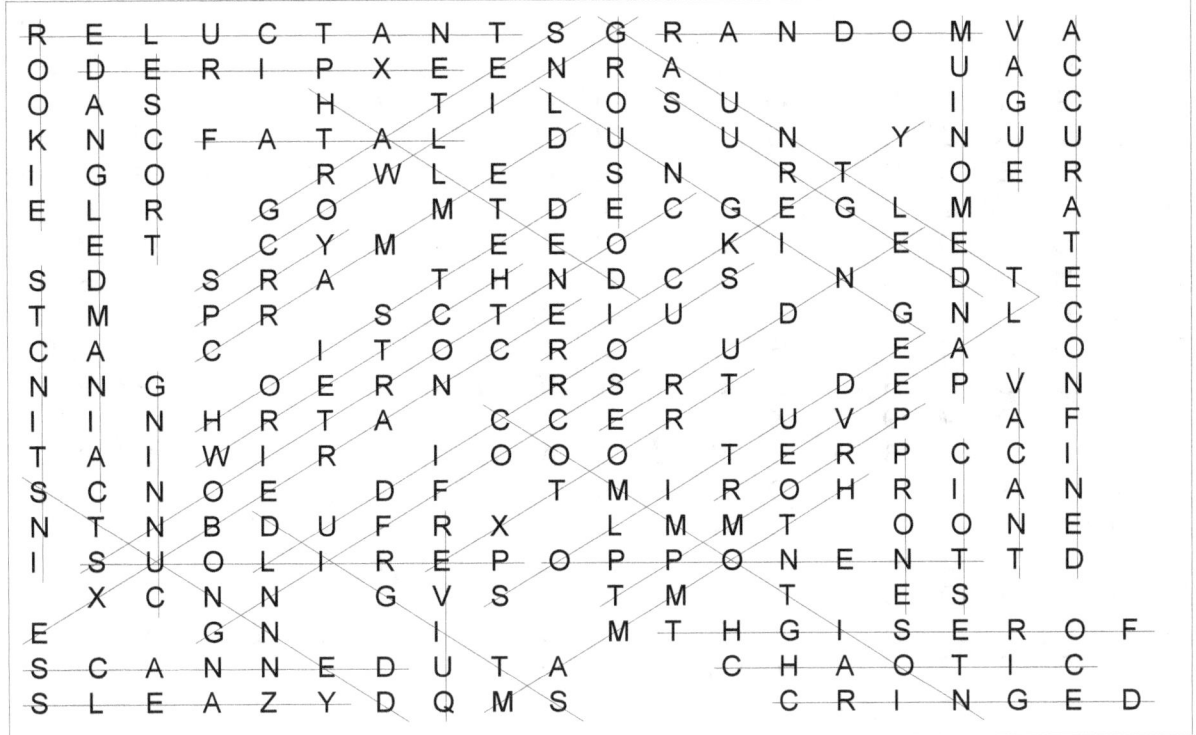

A first year player (6)
A guide or guard (6)
A miserable, unfortunate person (6)
A person who has extra enthusiasm or desire (6)
Aloneness (8)
An attack from all sides (8)
Complain; grumble (6)
Crowded; packed (7)
Dangerous (8)
Deadly (5)
Disorderly (7)
Disturbance (9)
Empty (6)
Ended (7)
Enthusiasm (10)
Exactly correct (8)
Flat (5)
Gigantic; enormous (7)
Having no pattern or purpose (6)
Having skill in deception (7)
Hung loosely (7)
Indifferent to pain or pleasure (5)
Instant; immediate (6)
Jeering (8)
Lifted (7)

Limited (8)
Looked over quickly (7)
Looking into the future (9)
Make known (6)
Moved like waves (6)
Moving forward suddenly (7)
Natural impulses or motivations (9)
Number symbols (6)
One against another (8)
Parallel bars for blocking an opening (6)
Ridiculous (9)
Shabby and dirty (6)
Shaky (7)
Shocked (7)
Stopped (6)
To bear with tolerance (6)
To force open or up (3)
To get by threats (6)
To shake with a slight movement (6)
Twisting and bending out of shape (11)
Unspecified; unclear (5)
Unwilling (9)
Uproar; confusion (11)
Winced; recoiled (7)
Wrinkling the forehead in anger (8)

Maniac Magee Vocabulary Word Search 2

```
M A M M O T H D E M M A R C D W W D A X
T T D H C T E R W W P A G E L Z N E C N
T Q E L B L L Q N R D F N H G M E H C N
R C T B Z D Y U F E M N I I O N S C U S
N C S Z G P P T R N A I G D A D U N R C
Q U I V E R E L U C T A N T V C O E A F
N R O X O Y A N S H H A U U S I R L T Y
G N H M T R O T X E R I L H T N G C E S
F X P C C V I H E D S W N O R E V E A L
P T D A N G L E D S W T M G V G L D P W
S C E U I B J L G B N M O A N A E Y P R
E R R D M D E K M E O D C I S H G H A G
E I U R E B Y C N C D A N E C K S U R B
T N T X B X F O S E N N R N O F T R E J
H G N B X Y P O N T U K I D F A U A N S
I E E N Z P R I U C A L K U F T N N T S
N D V A O C F T R N F T N R I A N T L T
G T E L T N U A G E D S I E N L E I Y F
G L P R O N E Y W L D E S C G T D N B D
S B K C H A L T E D F J D Z S U R G E D
```

A miserable, unfortunate person (6)
A person who has extra enthusiasm or desire (6)
Amazed; astonished (11)
An attack from all sides (8)
Complain; grumble (6)
Concerned with small details (8)
Crowded; packed (7)
Deadly (5)
Disturbance (9)
Easily understood (10)
Empty (6)
Ended (7)
Exactly correct (8)
Flat (5)
Gigantic; enormous (7)
Grasped tightly (8)
Having no pattern or purpose (6)
Having skill in deception (7)
Hung loosely (7)
Indifferent to pain or pleasure (5)
Instant; immediate (6)
Jeering (8)
Lifted (7)
Limited (8)
Looked over quickly (7)

Make known (6)
Moved like waves (6)
Moving forward suddenly (7)
Number symbols (6)
One against another (8)
Overjoyed (8)
Parallel bars for blocking an opening (6)
Rolling or pitching suddenly (8)
Shabby and dirty (6)
Shocked (7)
Shrank back in fear (8)
Speaking in a violent manner (7)
Stopped (6)
Streaked with gray (8)
To bear with tolerance (6)
To force open or up (3)
To get by threats (6)
To shake with a slight movement (6)
Twisted (8)
Unspecified; unclear (5)
Unwilling (9)
Violently excited (8)
Went in spite of risk (8)
Winced; recoiled (7)

Maniac Magee Vocabulary Word Search 2 Answer Key

A miserable, unfortunate person (6)
A person who has extra enthusiasm or desire (6)
Amazed; astonished (11)
An attack from all sides (8)
Complain; grumble (6)
Concerned with small details (8)
Crowded; packed (7)
Deadly (5)
Disturbance (9)
Easily understood (10)
Empty (6)
Ended (7)
Exactly correct (8)
Flat (5)
Gigantic; enormous (7)
Grasped tightly (8)
Having no pattern or purpose (6)
Having skill in deception (7)
Hung loosely (7)
Indifferent to pain or pleasure (5)
Instant; immediate (6)
Jeering (8)
Lifted (7)
Limited (8)
Looked over quickly (7)
Make known (6)
Moved like waves (6)
Moving forward suddenly (7)
Number symbols (6)
One against another (8)
Overjoyed (8)
Parallel bars for blocking an opening (6)
Rolling or pitching suddenly (8)
Shabby and dirty (6)
Shocked (7)
Shrank back in fear (8)
Speaking in a violent manner (7)
Stopped (6)
Streaked with gray (8)
To bear with tolerance (6)
To force open or up (3)
To get by threats (6)
To shake with a slight movement (6)
Twisted (8)
Unspecified; unclear (5)
Unwilling (9)
Violently excited (8)
Went in spite of risk (8)
Winced; recoiled (7)

91
Copyrighted

Maniac Magee Vocabulary Word Search 3

```
R A C V E S C O R T G W P P S P D D F W
E P H Z E T D Y J N D R Z R O F E E A N
P P A D W N T A I J E E S O L R L T A T
R A O Q E G T L N P B N K M I G Z L A P
I R T D B S W U O G Y C Z P T A Z A L N
S E I E O O O S R Z L H X T U I H U D
A N C T C P T L A E S E K C D N R C N F
L T D S G E P E A T D D D A E T G O G Y
S L E I R M L O I T N A C A V L L N I T
P Y X O O S D G N X I C C G T E U T N S
Q S U H U Y I R S E U O C R H T D O G G
N S B I S D H A C R N Y N A G B I R S W
T U E N E S S N A F C T S T I L C T G J
Z R R C V K N T N L S E T E S O R I B R
R G A U R K E I N I U K C S E B O O L Q
E E N B V A T N E N O C N R V U N B V
V D C A T A M G D C L I I E O I S S N C
E M E T Y R G M L H I R T V F O D O O C
A K A I A G W U E E R W S I K U I H I S
L C O N V E R G E D E N N U T S E T T G
Z K D G I C E X M X P I I Q U I A O O X
L O G R H A T C X R C S W L K T I M M R
M L S I G O C Q C K G M L O S C Z M M H
M Q N P R Y H F Y Q L I O C Z R P A O P
N G M T C R I N G E D R E N O R P M C V
```

ACCURATE	EXUBERANCE	LUNGING	REVEAL
APPARENTLY	FATAL	LURCHING	RICKETY
CHAOTIC	FINICKY	MAMMOTH	ROOKIE
COMMOTION	FLINCHED	MANIAC	SCANNED
CONTORTIONS	FORESIGHT	OBVIOUS	SCOWLING
CONVERGED	GAUNTLET	OPPONENT	SLEAZY
CRAMMED	GRATES	PERILOUS	SOLITUDE
CRINGED	GRIZZLED	PREPOSTEROUS	STOIC
DANGLED	GROUSE	PROMPT	STUNNED
DESOLATION	HALTED	PRONE	SURGED
DIGITS	HOISTED	PRY	VACANT
ECSTATIC	ILLUSION	QUIVER	VAGUE
ESCORT	INCUBATING	RANDOM	VENTURED
EXPIRED	INSTINCTS	RANTING	WRENCHED
EXTORT	LUDICROUS	REPRISALS	WRETCH

Maniac Magee Vocabulary Word Search 3 Answer Key

[Word search grid with letters arranged in a puzzle with solution lines drawn through found words]

ACCURATE	EXUBERANCE	LUNGING	REVEAL
APPARENTLY	FATAL	LURCHING	RICKETY
CHAOTIC	FINICKY	MAMMOTH	ROOKIE
COMMOTION	FLINCHED	MANIAC	SCANNED
CONTORTIONS	FORESIGHT	OBVIOUS	SCOWLING
CONVERGED	GAUNTLET	OPPONENT	SLEAZY
CRAMMED	GRATES	PERILOUS	SOLITUDE
CRINGED	GRIZZLED	PREPOSTEROUS	STOIC
DANGLED	GROUSE	PROMPT	STUNNED
DESOLATION	HALTED	PRONE	SURGED
DIGITS	HOISTED	PRY	VACANT
ECSTATIC	ILLUSION	QUIVER	VAGUE
ESCORT	INCUBATING	RANDOM	VENTURED
EXPIRED	INSTINCTS	RANTING	WRENCHED
EXTORT	LUDICROUS	REPRISALS	WRETCH

Maniac Magee Vocabulary Word Search 4

O	B	V	I	O	U	S	N	O	I	T	R	O	T	N	O	C	C	M	L		
R	W	C	N	D	G	R	O	U	S	E	P	J	J	D	L	H	S	A	Y		
Y	J	D	F	E	Q	D	I	O	T	N	B	R	E	P	A	A	E	N	Y		
Y	X	N	A	S	V	E	T	P	Q	H	R	R	O	A	E	O	C	I	J		
M	A	M	M	O	T	H	O	P	T	U	I	Y	C	N	V	T	S	A	X		
P	V	Q	O	L	V	C	M	O	F	P	I	C	W	L	E	I	T	C	G		
W	R	X	U	A	B	N	M	N	X	K	U	V	K	R	R	C	A	S	W		
L	D	E	S	T	H	I	O	E	D	R	J	L	E	Q	E	F	T	E	C		
R	M	D	P	I	D	L	C	N	A	V	Q	B	U	R	I	T	I	E	G		
R	A	N	D	O	M	F	A	T	A	L	G	N	I	N	N	U	C	T	D		
C	T	M	P	N	S	G	E	S	D	R	M	C	I	M	G	O	P	H	Q		
D	R	X	R	D	Y	T	K	N	A	P	I	C	L	T	M	I	A	I	E		
C	F	A	O	I	I	M	E	T	E	O	K	S	K	P	D	E	N	N	R		
V	W	C	M	L	N	G	E	R	T	Y	H	A	L	T	E	D	D	G	Q		
A	E	O	U	L	M	R	S	I	O	W	J	I	U	K	G	U	E	N	N		
C	V	N	T	N	R	S	L	T	J	U	M	Y	D	Y	R	T	M	I	T		
A	S	V	I	J	E	L	D	V	I	S	E	N	I	E	U	I	O	H	R		
N	C	E	X	U	B	E	R	A	N	C	E	D	C	I	S	L	N	C	Z		
T	A	R	S	H	R	E	J	T	M	C	E	F	R	K	T	O	I	R	C		
P	N	G	I	D	O	E	S	X	T	L	T	A	O	O	U	S	U	U	B		
R	E	N	V	N	Y	I	D	C	Z	V	N	S	U	O	N	R	M	L	M		
Y	E	D	A	L	G	C	S	Z	O	T	R	H	S	R	N	R	M	S	W		
S	D	X	G	S	H	E	I	T	I	R	R	I	C	K	E	T	Y	W	C		
G	V	G	U	J	P	R	D	N	E	X	T	O	R	T	D	V	P	K	F		
K	S	J	E	R	G	P	G	J	T	D	R	E	P	R	I	S	A	L	S		

ACCURATE	EXTORT	MAMMOTH	RICKETY
CHAOTIC	EXUBERANCE	MANIAC	ROOKIE
COMMOTION	FATAL	OBVIOUS	SCANNED
COMPLIMENTS	FINICKY	OPPONENT	SEETHING
CONTORTIONS	FLINCHED	PANDEMONIUM	SOLITUDE
CONVERGED	GRATES	PERILOUS	STOIC
CRAMMED	GRIZZLED	PREPOSTEROUS	STUNNED
CRINGED	GROUSE	PROMPT	SURGED
CUNNING	HALTED	PRONE	VACANT
DESOLATION	HOISTED	PRY	VAGUE
DIGITS	INFAMOUS	QUIVER	VENTURED
ECSTATIC	INSTINCTS	RANDOM	WRETCH
ENDURE	LUDICROUS	RANTING	
ESCORT	LUNGING	REPRISALS	
EXPIRED	LURCHING	REVEAL	

Maniac Magee Vocabulary Word Search 4 Answer Key

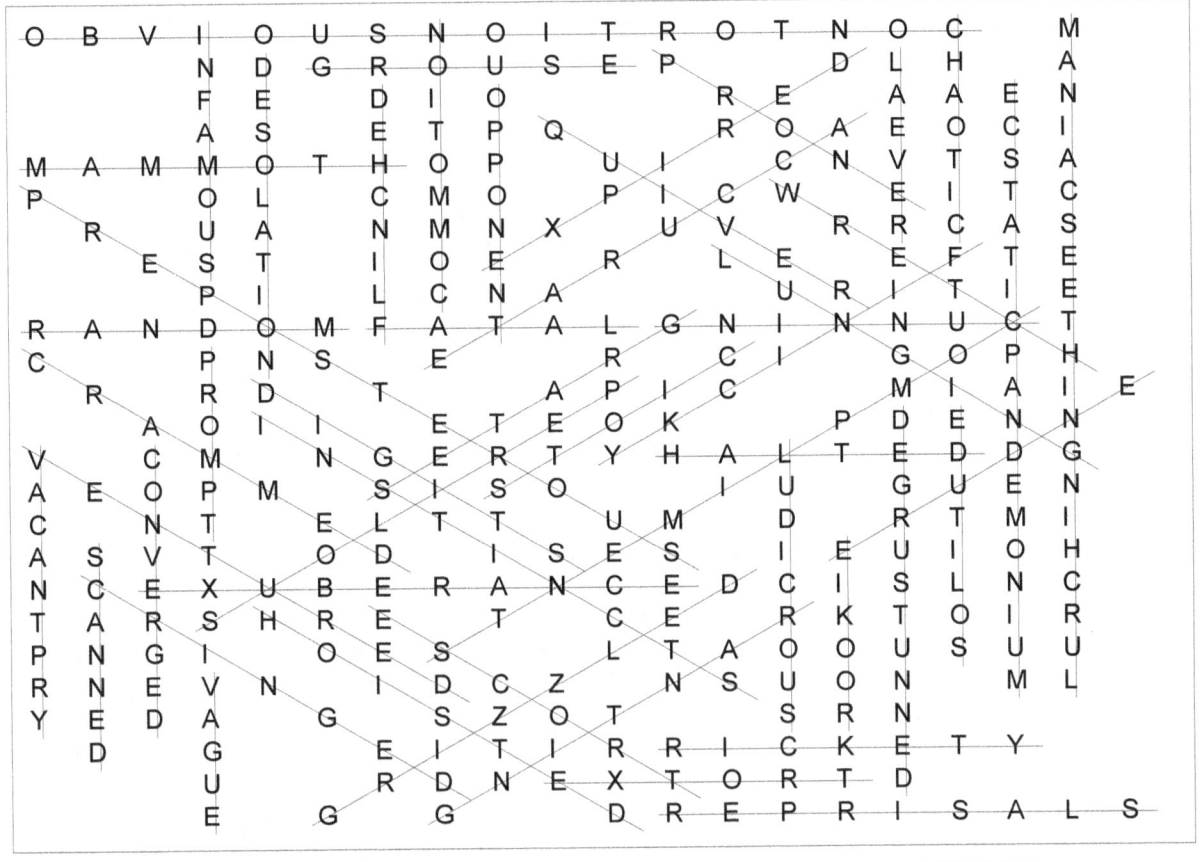

ACCURATE	EXTORT	MAMMOTH	RICKETY
CHAOTIC	EXUBERANCE	MANIAC	ROOKIE
COMMOTION	FATAL	OBVIOUS	SCANNED
COMPLIMENTS	FINICKY	OPPONENT	SEETHING
CONTORTIONS	FLINCHED	PANDEMONIUM	SOLITUDE
CONVERGED	GRATES	PERILOUS	STOIC
CRAMMED	GRIZZLED	PREPOSTEROUS	STUNNED
CRINGED	GROUSE	PROMPT	SURGED
CUNNING	HALTED	PRONE	VACANT
DESOLATION	HOISTED	PRY	VAGUE
DIGITS	INFAMOUS	QUIVER	VENTURED
ECSTATIC	INSTINCTS	RANDOM	WRETCH
ENDURE	LUDICROUS	RANTING	
ESCORT	LUNGING	REPRISALS	
EXPIRED	LURCHING	REVEAL	

Maniac Magee Vocabulary Crossword 1

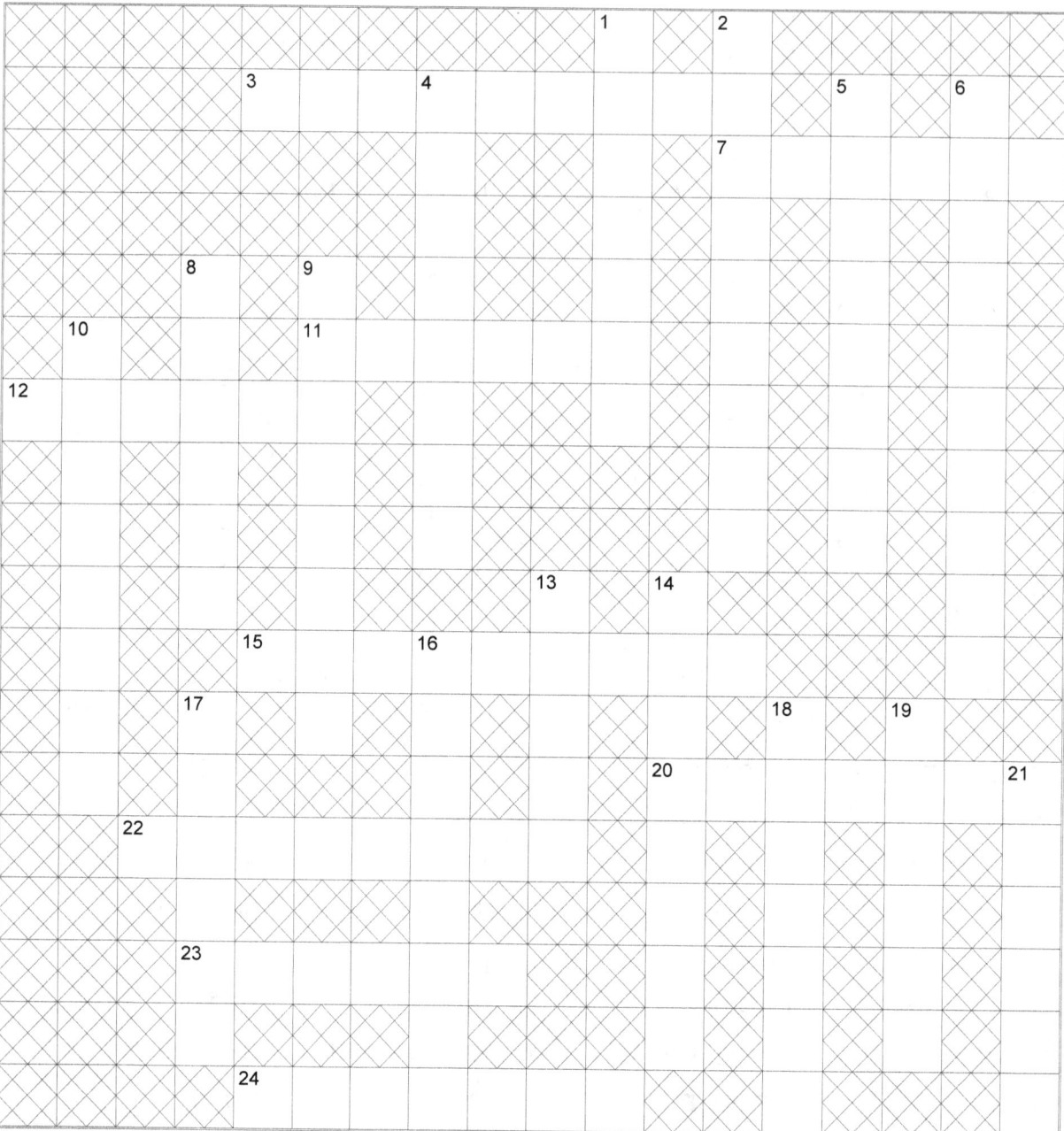

Across
3. Disturbance
7. Moved like waves
11. To get by threats
12. To shake with a slight movement
15. Ridiculous
20. Shocked
22. Exactly correct
23. Having no pattern or purpose
24. Lifted

Down
1. Shaky
2. Natural impulses or motivations
4. Concerned with small details
5. Streaked with gray
6. Gloom; bleakness
8. Make known
9. Dangerous
10. Rolling or pitching suddenly
13. Flat
14. Followers trying to overtake; chasers
16. Having a very bad reputation
17. A guide or guard
18. Having skill in deception
19. To bear with tolerance
21. Number symbols

Maniac Magee Vocabulary Crossword 1 Answer Key

Across
- 3. Disturbance
- 7. Moved like waves
- 11. To get by threats
- 12. To shake with a slight movement
- 15. Ridiculous
- 20. Shocked
- 22. Exactly correct
- 23. Having no pattern or purpose
- 24. Lifted

Down
- 1. Shaky
- 2. Natural impulses or motivations
- 4. Concerned with small details
- 5. Streaked with gray
- 6. Gloom; bleakness
- 8. Make known
- 9. Dangerous
- 10. Rolling or pitching suddenly
- 13. Flat
- 14. Followers trying to overtake; chasers
- 16. Having a very bad reputation
- 17. A guide or guard
- 18. Having skill in deception
- 19. To bear with tolerance
- 21. Number symbols

Maniac Magee Vocabulary Crossword 2

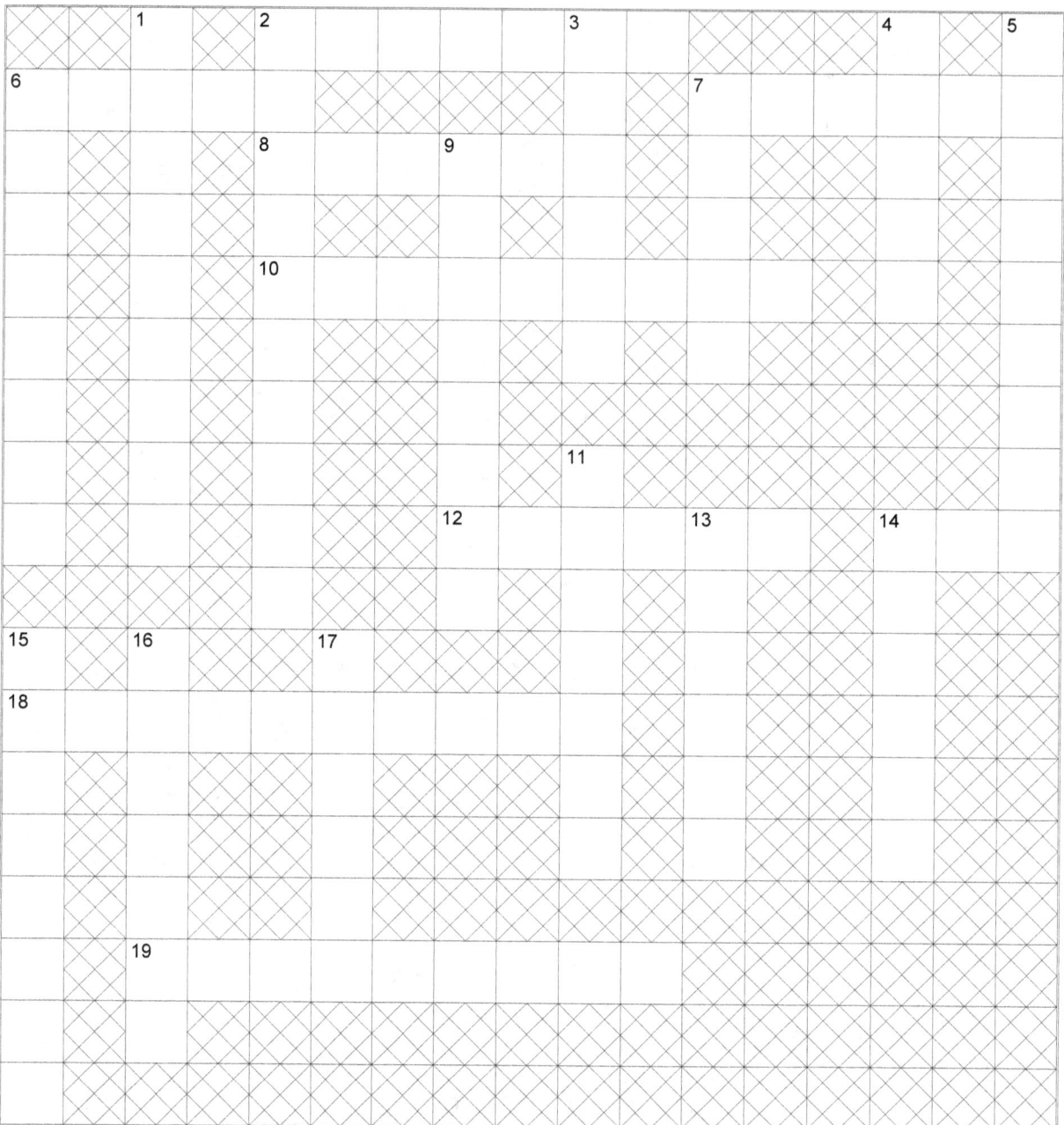

Across
2. Hung loosely
6. Flat
7. Empty
8. Moved like waves
10. Ridiculous
12. To get by threats
14. To force open or up
18. Complete weariness
19. Natural impulses or motivations

Down
1. Disturbance
2. Gloom; bleakness
3. To bear with tolerance
4. Deadly
5. Dependability
6. Dangerous
7. Unspecified; unclear
9. Streaked with gray
11. Shocked
13. Make known
14. Instant; immediate
15. Violently excited
16. Disorderly
17. A guide or guard

Maniac Magee Vocabulary Crossword 2 Answer Key

Across
- 2. Hung loosely
- 6. Flat
- 7. Empty
- 8. Moved like waves
- 10. Ridiculous
- 12. To get by threats
- 14. To force open or up
- 18. Complete weariness
- 19. Natural impulses or motivations

Down
- 1. Disturbance
- 2. Gloom; bleakness
- 3. To bear with tolerance
- 4. Deadly
- 5. Dependability
- 6. Dangerous
- 7. Unspecified; unclear
- 9. Streaked with gray
- 11. Shocked
- 13. Make known
- 14. Instant; immediate
- 15. Violently excited
- 16. Disorderly
- 17. A guide or guard

Maniac Magee Vocabulary Crossword 3

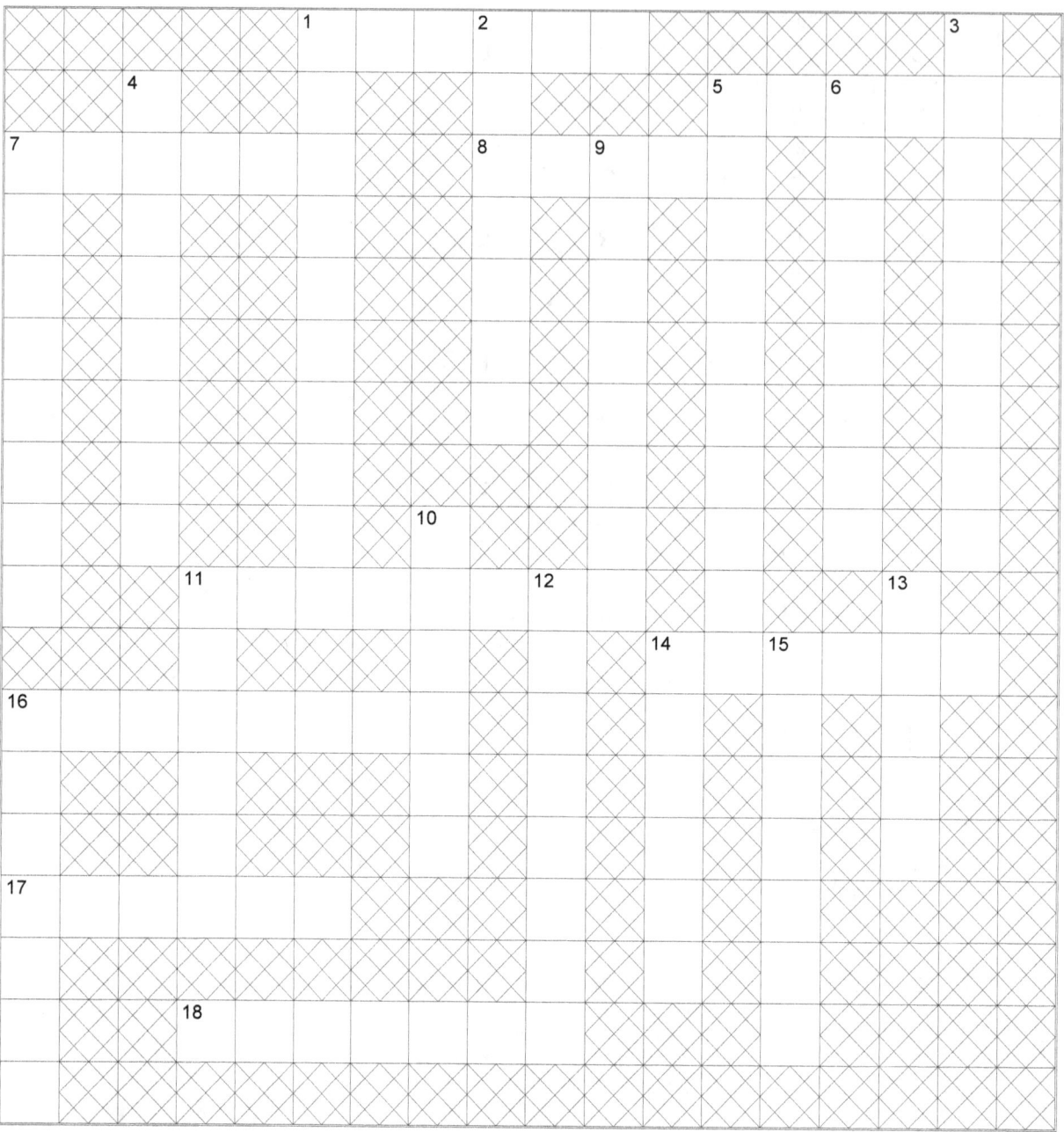

Across
1. To get by threats
5. Number symbols
7. A miserable, unfortunate person
8. Unspecified; unclear
11. Went in spite of risk
14. To bear with tolerance
16. Rolling or pitching suddenly
17. Parallel bars for blocking an opening
18. Disorderly

Down
1. Complete weariness
2. Apparent; observable
3. Dependability
4. Dangerous
5. Gloom; bleakness
6. An attack from all sides
7. Twisted
9. Streaked with gray
10. Moved like waves
11. Empty
12. Overjoyed
13. Flat
14. A guide or guard
15. Hung loosely
16. Moving forward suddenly

Maniac Magee Vocabulary Crossword 3 Answer Key

				¹E	²T	O	R	T			³S	
		⁴P		X		B			⁵D	⁶G	T	S
⁷W	R	E	T	C	H	⁸V	A	⁹G	U	E	A	
R		R		A		I		R		S	U	B
E		I		U		O		I		O	N	I
N		L		S		U		Z		L	T	L
C		O		T		S		Z		A	L	I
H		U		I				L		T	E	T
E		S		O	¹⁰S			E		I	T	Y
D		¹¹V	E	N	T	U	R	E	D	O	¹³P	
		A			R		C	¹⁴E	¹⁵N	D	U	R	E
¹⁶L	U	R	C	H	I	N	G	S	C	A	O	
U		A			E		T	C	N	N		
N		N			D		A	O	G	E		
¹⁷G	R	A	T	E	S		T	R	L			
I							I	T	E			
N		¹⁸C	H	A	O	T	I	C	D			
G												

Across
1. To get by threats
5. Number symbols
7. A miserable, unfortunate person
8. Unspecified; unclear
11. Went in spite of risk
14. To bear with tolerance
16. Rolling or pitching suddenly
17. Parallel bars for blocking an opening
18. Disorderly

Down
1. Complete weariness
2. Apparent; observable
3. Dependability
4. Dangerous
5. Gloom; bleakness
6. An attack from all sides
7. Twisted
9. Streaked with gray
10. Moved like waves
11. Empty
12. Overjoyed
13. Flat
14. A guide or guard
15. Hung loosely
16. Moving forward suddenly

Maniac Magee Vocabulary Crossword 4

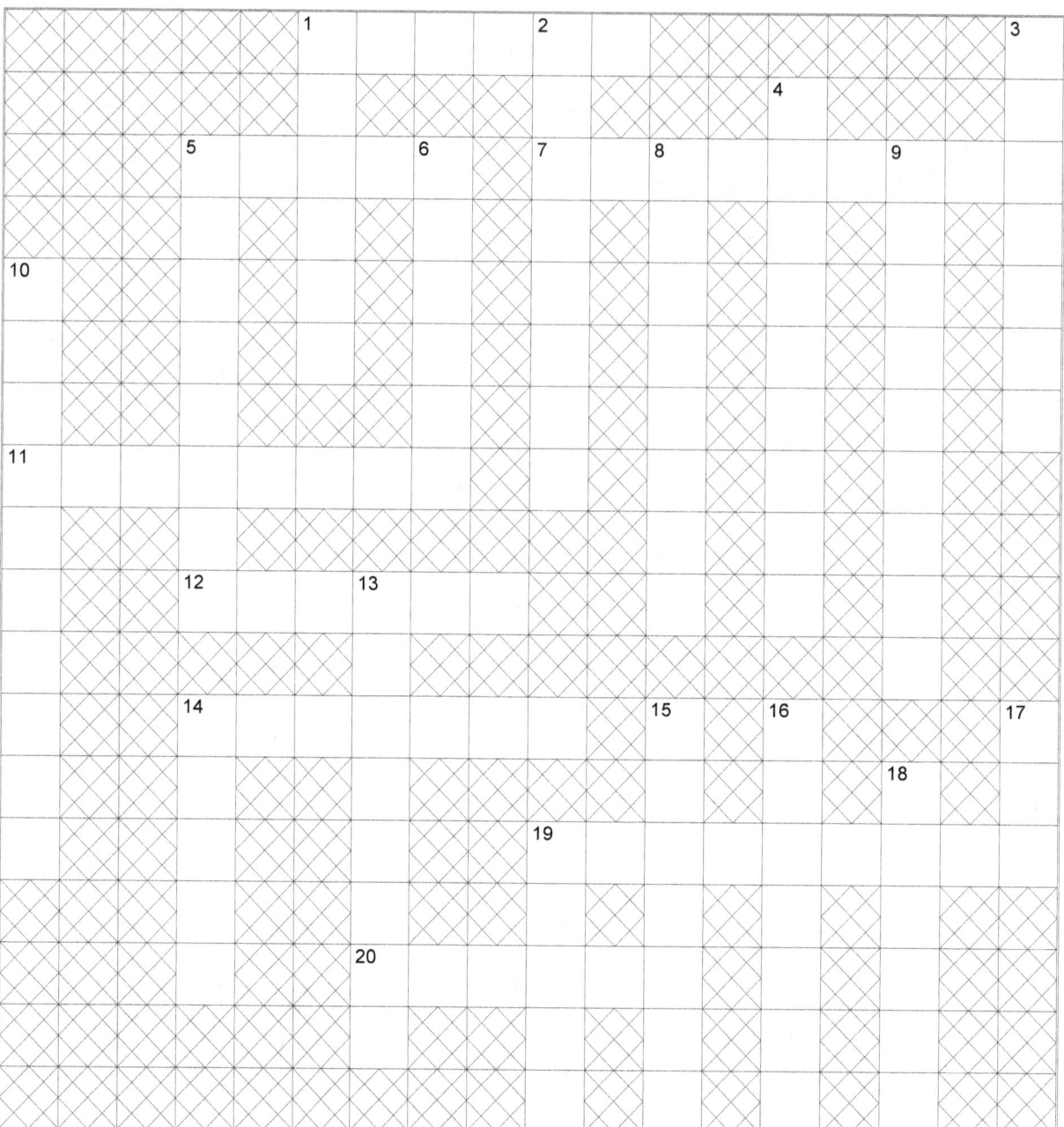

Across
1. Make known
5. Flat
7. Disturbance
11. One against another
12. Moved like waves
14. Choosy; fussy
19. Dependability
20. To get by threats

Down
1. A first year player
2. Exactly correct
3. Hung loosely
4. Looking into the future
5. Dangerous
6. A guide or guard
8. Concerned with small details
9. Natural impulses or motivations
10. Gloom; bleakness
13. Streaked with gray
14. Deadly
15. Disorderly
16. Winced; recoiled
17. To force open or up
18. Number symbols
19. Indifferent to pain or pleasure

Maniac Magee Vocabulary Crossword 4 Answer Key

				1 R	E	V	2 A	L				3 D
				O			C			4 F		A
			5 P	R	6 O	N	7 E		8 C	O	M	M	9 O	T	I	O	N
			E		K		S		U		I		R		N		G
10 D		R		I		C		R		N		E		S		L
E		I		E		O		A		U		S		T		E
S		L				R		T		T		I		I		D
11 O	P	P	O	N	E	N	T		E		E		G		N	
L			U							L		H		C	
A		12 S	U	R	13 G	E	D			Y		T		T	
T					R									S	
I		14 F	I	N	I	C	K	Y	15 C		16 C			17 P
O		A			Z				H		R		18 D		R
N		T			Z		19 S	T	A	B	I	L	I	T	Y
		A			L		T		O		N		G		
		L		20 E	X	T	O	R	T		G		I		
				D			I		I		E		T		
							C		C		D		S		

Across
1. Make known
5. Flat
7. Disturbance
11. One against another
12. Moved like waves
14. Choosy; fussy
19. Dependability
20. To get by threats

Down
1. A first year player
2. Exactly correct
3. Hung loosely
4. Looking into the future
5. Dangerous
6. A guide or guard
8. Concerned with small details
9. Natural impulses or motivations
10. Gloom; bleakness
13. Streaked with gray
14. Deadly
15. Disorderly
16. Winced; recoiled
17. To force open or up
18. Number symbols
19. Indifferent to pain or pleasure

Maniac Magee Vocabulary Juggle Letters 1

1. SOEGRU = 1. _____
   Complain; grumble

2. NGFCFISO = 2. _____
   Jeering

3. DETNSNU = 3. _____
   Shocked

4. VIERQU = 4. _____
   To shake with a slight movement

5. DMECAMR = 5. _____
   Crowded; packed

6. NCEAERUBXE = 6. _____
   Enthusiasm

7. SSNICTITN = 7. _____
   Natural impulses or motivations

8. NRDMOA = 8. _____
   Having no pattern or purpose

9. DRCEHNWE = 9. _____
   Twisted

10. UGHIRCNL = 10. _____
    Rolling or pitching suddenly

11. ATCISETC = 11. _____
    Overjoyed

12. TYBLSAITI = 12. _____
    Dependability

13. MEISTOCMPNL = 13. _____
    Acts of courtesy

14. TERCSO = 14. _____
    A guide or guard

15. TSAODINOLE = 15. _____
    Gloom; bleakness

Maniac Magee Vocabulary Juggle Letters 1 Answer Key

1. SOEGRU = 1. GROUSE
   Complain; grumble

2. NGFCFISO = 2. SCOFFING
   Jeering

3. DETNSNU = 3. STUNNED
   Shocked

4. VIERQU = 4. QUIVER
   To shake with a slight movement

5. DMECAMR = 5. CRAMMED
   Crowded; packed

6. NCEAERUBXE = 6. EXUBERANCE
   Enthusiasm

7. SSNICTITN = 7. INSTINCTS
   Natural impulses or motivations

8. NRDMOA = 8. RANDOM
   Having no pattern or purpose

9. DRCEHNWE = 9. WRENCHED
   Twisted

10. UGHIRCNL = 10. LURCHING
    Rolling or pitching suddenly

11. ATCISETC = 11. ECSTATIC
    Overjoyed

12. TYBLSAITI = 12. STABILITY
    Dependability

13. MEISTOCMPNL = 13. COMPLIMENTS
    Acts of courtesy

14. TERCSO = 14. ESCORT
    A guide or guard

15. TSAODINOLE = 15. DESOLATION
    Gloom; bleakness

Maniac Magee Vocabulary Juggle Letters 2

1. SIUBOOV = 1. _____
   Apparent; observable

2. NCLHDCEE = 2. _____
   Grasped tightly

3. DRMCMEA = 3. _____
   Crowded; packed

4. EHALTD = 4. _____
   Stopped

5. NOTSNORCOIT = 5. _____
   Twisting and bending out of shape

6. OIILNULS = 6. _____
   Fantasy; false belief

7. RGOUSE = 7. _____
   Complain; grumble

8. IAACMN = 8. _____
   A person who has extra enthusiasm or desire

9. HOEFRIGST = 9. _____
   Looking into the future

10. XNTESIUHAO =10. _____
    Complete weariness

11. UNMPAMDOINE =11. _____
    Uproar; confusion

12. NGSFOCFI =12. _____
    Jeering

13. TIAYLSITB =13. _____
    Dependability

14. NURDEE =14. _____
    To bear with tolerance

15. ENUTTLRAC =15. _____
    Unwilling

Maniac Magee Vocabulary Juggle Letters 2 Answer Key

1. SIUBOOV = 1. OBVIOUS
Apparent; observable

2. NCLHDCEE = 2. CLENCHED
Grasped tightly

3. DRMCMEA = 3. CRAMMED
Crowded; packed

4. EHALTD = 4. HALTED
Stopped

5. NOTSNORCOIT = 5. CONTORTIONS
Twisting and bending out of shape

6. OIILNULS = 6. ILLUSION
Fantasy; false belief

7. RGOUSE = 7. GROUSE
Complain; grumble

8. IAACMN = 8. MANIAC
A person who has extra enthusiasm or desire

9. HOEFRIGST = 9. FORESIGHT
Looking into the future

10. XNTESIUHAO = 10. EXHAUSTION
Complete weariness

11. UNMPAMDOINE = 11. PANDEMONIUM
Uproar; confusion

12. NGSFOCFI = 12. SCOFFING
Jeering

13. TIAYLSITB = 13. STABILITY
Dependability

14. NURDEE = 14. ENDURE
To bear with tolerance

15. ENUTTLRAC = 15. RELUCTANT
Unwilling

Maniac Magee Vocabulary Juggle Letters 3

1. GFFCNISO = 1. _____
   Jeering

2. OLIUINLS = 2. _____
   Fantasy; false belief

3. ANRGNIT = 3. _____
   Speaking in a violent manner

4. ASPSRRILE = 4. _____
   Revenge

5. DLTEAH = 5. _____
   Stopped

6. LIENRNBDGU = 6. _____
   Moving in a clumsy way

7. RCMADME = 7. _____
   Crowded; packed

8. RETAACUC = 8. _____
   Exactly correct

9. UUDBODFEDNM = 9. _____
   Amazed; astonished

10. NESNTDU = 10. _____
    Shocked

11. DEERUN = 11. _____
    To bear with tolerance

12. DNORMA = 12. _____
    Having no pattern or purpose

13. NRXEBUAEEC = 13. _____
    Enthusiasm

14. ODNECIFN = 14. _____
    Limited

15. SHLDNAEIUG = 15. _____
    Weakened; faded

Maniac Magee Vocabulary Juggle Letters 3 Answer Key

1. GFFCNISO = 1. SCOFFING
   Jeering

2. OLIUINLS = 2. ILLUSION
   Fantasy; false belief

3. ANRGNIT = 3. RANTING
   Speaking in a violent manner

4. ASPSRRILE = 4. REPRISALS
   Revenge

5. DLTEAH = 5. HALTED
   Stopped

6. LIENRNBDGU = 6. BLUNDERING
   Moving in a clumsy way

7. RCMADME = 7. CRAMMED
   Crowded; packed

8. RETAACUC = 8. ACCURATE
   Exactly correct

9. UUDBODFEDNM = 9. DUMBFOUNDED
   Amazed; astonished

10. NESNTDU =10. STUNNED
    Shocked

11. DEERUN =11. ENDURE
    To bear with tolerance

12. DNORMA =12. RANDOM
    Having no pattern or purpose

13. NRXEBUAEEC =13. EXUBERANCE
    Enthusiasm

14. ODNECIFN =14. CONFINED
    Limited

15. SHLDNAEIUG =15. LANGUISHED
    Weakened; faded

Maniac Magee Vocabulary Juggle Letters 4

1. EOUSGR = 1. _____
   Complain; grumble

2. ERUVIQ = 2. _____
   To shake with a slight movement

3. IXPDEER = 3. _____
   Ended

4. EAGUV = 4. _____
   Unspecified; unclear

5. ULUISODCR = 5. _____
   Ridiculous

6. FIIKNYC = 6. _____
   Choosy; fussy

7. MMAMHOT = 7. _____
   Gigantic; enormous

8. DOCNEVERG = 8. _____
   Came together

9. EUDSGR = 9. _____
   Moved like waves

10. ADEMCRM =10. _____
    Crowded; packed

11. OURSEOPTESPR =11. _____
    Farfetched

12. OMTOCIONM =12. _____
    Disturbance

13. NUTNDSE =13. _____
    Shocked

14. ECNCEHLD =14. _____
    Grasped tightly

15. OVIUBSO =15. _____
    Apparent; observable

Maniac Magee Vocabulary Juggle Letters 4 Answer Key

1. EOUSGR = 1. GROUSE
   Complain; grumble

2. ERUVIQ = 2. QUIVER
   To shake with a slight movement

3. IXPDEER = 3. EXPIRED
   Ended

4. EAGUV = 4. VAGUE
   Unspecified; unclear

5. ULUISODCR = 5. LUDICROUS
   Ridiculous

6. FIIKNYC = 6. FINICKY
   Choosy; fussy

7. MMAMHOT = 7. MAMMOTH
   Gigantic; enormous

8. DOCNEVERG = 8. CONVERGED
   Came together

9. EUDSGR = 9. SURGED
   Moved like waves

10. ADEMCRM = 10. CRAMMED
    Crowded; packed

11. OURSEOPTESPR = 11. PREPOSTEROUS
    Farfetched

12. OMTOCIONM = 12. COMMOTION
    Disturbance

13. NUTNDSE = 13. STUNNED
    Shocked

14. ECNCEHLD = 14. CLENCHED
    Grasped tightly

15. OVIUBSO = 15. OBVIOUS
    Apparent; observable

ACCURATE	Exactly correct
APPARENTLY	Easily understood
BELLOWING	Yelling
BLUNDERING	Moving in a clumsy way
CHAOTIC	Disorderly
CLENCHED	Grasped tightly

COMMOTION	Disturbance
COMPLIMENTS	Acts of courtesy
CONCLUSIONS	End results
CONFINED	Limited
CONTORTIONS	Twisting and bending out of shape
CONVERGED	Came together

CRAMMED	Crowded; packed
CRINGED	Winced; recoiled
CUNNING	Having skill in deception
DANGLED	Hung loosely
DESOLATION	Gloom; bleakness
DIGITS	Number symbols

DUMBFOUNDED	Amazed; astonished
ECSTATIC	Overjoyed
ENDURE	To bear with tolerance
ESCORT	A guide or guard
EXHAUSTION	Complete weariness
EXPIRED	Ended

EXTORT	To get by threats
EXUBERANCE	Enthusiasm
FATAL	Deadly
FINICKY	Choosy; fussy
FLINCHED	Shrank back in fear
FORESIGHT	Looking into the future

GAUNTLET	An attack from all sides
GRATES	Parallel bars for blocking an opening
GRIZZLED	Streaked with gray
GROUSE	Complain; grumble
HALTED	Stopped
HOISTED	Lifted

ILLUSION	Fantasy; false belief
INCUBATING	Developing and hatching
INFAMOUS	Having a very bad reputation
INSTINCTS	Natural impulses or motivations
LANGUISHED	Weakened; faded
LUDICROUS	Ridiculous

LUNGING	Moving forward suddenly
LURCHING	Rolling or pitching suddenly
MAMMOTH	Gigantic; enormous
MANIAC	A person who has extra enthusiasm or desire
MINUTELY	Concerned with small details
OBVIOUS	Apparent; observable

OPPONENT	One against another
PANDEMONIUM	Uproar; confusion
PERILOUS	Dangerous
PREPOSTEROUS	Farfetched
PROMPT	Instant; immediate
PRONE	Flat

PRY	To force open or up
PURSUERS	Followers trying to overtake; chasers
QUIVER	To shake with a slight movement
RANDOM	Having no pattern or purpose
RANTING	Speaking in a violent manner
RELUCTANT	Unwilling

REPRISALS	Revenge
REVEAL	Make known
RICKETY	Shaky
ROOKIE	A first year player
SCANNED	Looked over quickly
SCOFFING	Jeering

SCOWLING	Wrinkling the forehead in anger
SEETHING	Violently excited
SLEAZY	Shabby and dirty
SOLITUDE	Aloneness
STABILITY	Dependability
STOIC	Indifferent to pain or pleasure

STUNNED	Shocked
SURGED	Moved like waves
VACANT	Empty
VAGUE	Unspecified; unclear
VENTURED	Went in spite of risk
WRENCHED	Twisted

WRETCH

A miserable, unfortunate person

Maniac Magee Vocabulary

PANDEMONIUM	ACCURATE	SCOFFING	MANIAC	PRY
REPRISALS	CRAMMED	DESOLATION	EXHAUSTION	SEETHING
FORESIGHT	GRIZZLED	FREE SPACE	CRINGED	VENTURED
GAUNTLET	ROOKIE	ESCORT	INFAMOUS	DIGITS
CONTORTIONS	OPPONENT	RANTING	DUMBFOUNDED	HALTED

Maniac Magee Vocabulary

STABILITY	SCANNED	PURSUERS	PERILOUS	FINICKY
VAGUE	CONFINED	INCUBATING	RELUCTANT	HOISTED
FLINCHED	MAMMOTH	FREE SPACE	STUNNED	PREPOSTEROUS
QUIVER	ENDURE	MINUTELY	EXUBERANCE	COMPLIMENTS
WRETCH	RANDOM	CLENCHED	LURCHING	SCOWLING

Maniac Magee Vocabulary

GRATES	OPPONENT	WRETCH	SLEAZY	PERILOUS
FORESIGHT	VAGUE	DUMBFOUNDED	VENTURED	SCOFFING
COMPLIMENTS	EXTORT	FREE SPACE	EXHAUSTION	STABILITY
PURSUERS	QUIVER	DANGLED	BLUNDERING	LUDICROUS
EXUBERANCE	PRY	MAMMOTH	ECSTATIC	ESCORT

Maniac Magee Vocabulary

ILLUSION	PRONE	CONTORTIONS	PREPOSTEROUS	ROOKIE
GRIZZLED	RANTING	STOIC	SOLITUDE	PROMPT
RELUCTANT	LUNGING	FREE SPACE	FLINCHED	MINUTELY
STUNNED	CRAMMED	LANGUISHED	ENDURE	CONCLUSIONS
ACCURATE	INSTINCTS	INFAMOUS	REVEAL	SCOWLING

Maniac Magee Vocabulary

ECSTATIC	RANTING	RICKETY	RANDOM	FLINCHED
PERILOUS	LUNGING	ESCORT	EXTORT	REVEAL
CRAMMED	OPPONENT	FREE SPACE	CLENCHED	SCOWLING
CONFINED	BLUNDERING	CUNNING	SCOFFING	PRONE
CONTORTIONS	BELLOWING	MAMMOTH	VACANT	DANGLED

Maniac Magee Vocabulary

EXUBERANCE	GRIZZLED	PROMPT	LURCHING	SURGED
MANIAC	STOIC	OBVIOUS	CHAOTIC	PRY
FATAL	PANDEMONIUM	FREE SPACE	STABILITY	INCUBATING
PREPOSTEROUS	HOISTED	DESOLATION	SCANNED	HALTED
RELUCTANT	ENDURE	INSTINCTS	DUMBFOUNDED	INFAMOUS

Maniac Magee Vocabulary

FORESIGHT	MAMMOTH	ROOKIE	REPRISALS	CUNNING
PERILOUS	INCUBATING	ACCURATE	MANIAC	CRAMMED
SCOWLING	CONVERGED	FREE SPACE	SEETHING	DUMBFOUNDED
HOISTED	OBVIOUS	APPARENTLY	PRY	CLENCHED
EXTORT	DANGLED	COMMOTION	ECSTATIC	GAUNTLET

Maniac Magee Vocabulary

SCOFFING	RANTING	LUNGING	SOLITUDE	LANGUISHED
PURSUERS	REVEAL	STOIC	DIGITS	PRONE
DESOLATION	RELUCTANT	FREE SPACE	CONCLUSIONS	GRIZZLED
PANDEMONIUM	INSTINCTS	MINUTELY	STABILITY	ENDURE
SLEAZY	INFAMOUS	EXUBERANCE	CRINGED	PROMPT

Maniac Magee Vocabulary

SCOFFING	CONTORTIONS	HALTED	MANIAC	PROMPT
CONVERGED	PRONE	SLEAZY	BELLOWING	MINUTELY
VAGUE	FORESIGHT	FREE SPACE	DANGLED	PRY
SEETHING	CRAMMED	CONCLUSIONS	PERILOUS	RANDOM
EXUBERANCE	INCUBATING	RICKETY	CRINGED	STABILITY

Maniac Magee Vocabulary

EXHAUSTION	SCANNED	CLENCHED	ESCORT	COMMOTION
LUDICROUS	RELUCTANT	FLINCHED	WRENCHED	LUNGING
OPPONENT	GAUNTLET	FREE SPACE	ILLUSION	DUMBFOUNDED
CUNNING	BLUNDERING	REPRISALS	QUIVER	GRATES
EXPIRED	HOISTED	ECSTATIC	GROUSE	VENTURED

Maniac Magee Vocabulary

MANIAC	ESCORT	SCOWLING	SCANNED	STABILITY
MAMMOTH	SLEAZY	RICKETY	DUMBFOUNDED	CRINGED
RELUCTANT	GAUNTLET	FREE SPACE	PANDEMONIUM	ECSTATIC
BELLOWING	INCUBATING	EXUBERANCE	EXHAUSTION	CONFINED
BLUNDERING	HOISTED	VAGUE	GRIZZLED	VENTURED

Maniac Magee Vocabulary

QUIVER	RANDOM	ACCURATE	STOIC	PURSUERS
PRY	SEETHING	COMPLIMENTS	LANGUISHED	OBVIOUS
CLENCHED	FLINCHED	FREE SPACE	VACANT	SURGED
ENDURE	INSTINCTS	CONCLUSIONS	INFAMOUS	CHAOTIC
PROMPT	SOLITUDE	OPPONENT	FINICKY	DIGITS

Maniac Magee Vocabulary

REPRISALS	RICKETY	WRETCH	INFAMOUS	ENDURE
DIGITS	SLEAZY	RELUCTANT	PREPOSTEROUS	CRAMMED
SURGED	MINUTELY	FREE SPACE	FORESIGHT	BLUNDERING
SCANNED	PROMPT	STABILITY	EXUBERANCE	STOIC
OBVIOUS	MAMMOTH	SEETHING	RANDOM	CRINGED

Maniac Magee Vocabulary

PURSUERS	ILLUSION	DESOLATION	VACANT	SCOWLING
STUNNED	PERILOUS	FATAL	DANGLED	CHAOTIC
GAUNTLET	ROOKIE	FREE SPACE	REVEAL	ESCORT
PRONE	COMMOTION	INSTINCTS	ECSTATIC	DUMBFOUNDED
LANGUISHED	PANDEMONIUM	APPARENTLY	LUNGING	BELLOWING

Maniac Magee Vocabulary

RANDOM	ACCURATE	WRENCHED	REVEAL	GRATES
REPRISALS	ENDURE	ESCORT	STABILITY	OBVIOUS
DANGLED	CONTORTIONS	FREE SPACE	BELLOWING	VENTURED
LUDICROUS	SCANNED	QUIVER	FORESIGHT	WRETCH
DUMBFOUNDED	PERILOUS	RICKETY	MAMMOTH	LURCHING

Maniac Magee Vocabulary

CHAOTIC	SLEAZY	SURGED	VAGUE	EXPIRED
CRINGED	CONFINED	EXHAUSTION	MANIAC	COMPLIMENTS
OPPONENT	EXTORT	FREE SPACE	INSTINCTS	CLENCHED
ECSTATIC	HALTED	CRAMMED	STUNNED	SOLITUDE
PANDEMONIUM	SCOFFING	PURSUERS	RELUCTANT	SCOWLING

Maniac Magee Vocabulary

QUIVER	PURSUERS	FINICKY	INFAMOUS	CUNNING
WRETCH	LUDICROUS	WRENCHED	CONTORTIONS	PREPOSTEROUS
SCANNED	CHAOTIC	FREE SPACE	REPRISALS	GAUNTLET
CRINGED	EXUBERANCE	RANDOM	STABILITY	COMPLIMENTS
REVEAL	FLINCHED	INSTINCTS	SCOWLING	SEETHING

Maniac Magee Vocabulary

PRY	MAMMOTH	RANTING	GROUSE	VAGUE
MINUTELY	SLEAZY	HOISTED	SURGED	MANIAC
DUMBFOUNDED	BELLOWING	FREE SPACE	DESOLATION	EXPIRED
VACANT	DANGLED	LURCHING	LUNGING	GRIZZLED
GRATES	HALTED	INCUBATING	STOIC	EXTORT

Maniac Magee Vocabulary

MAMMOTH	CONVERGED	RANTING	REPRISALS	SURGED
LUNGING	DESOLATION	RANDOM	OBVIOUS	STOIC
PERILOUS	FORESIGHT	FREE SPACE	RICKETY	PREPOSTEROUS
CRAMMED	INCUBATING	LANGUISHED	SCOWLING	LUDICROUS
DANGLED	MANIAC	CONFINED	SOLITUDE	VENTURED

Maniac Magee Vocabulary

SCOFFING	GROUSE	GRIZZLED	EXPIRED	MINUTELY
STUNNED	INSTINCTS	DUMBFOUNDED	ESCORT	CONTORTIONS
QUIVER	GAUNTLET	FREE SPACE	ILLUSION	PURSUERS
SEETHING	SLEAZY	FLINCHED	EXUBERANCE	BLUNDERING
ROOKIE	ENDURE	INFAMOUS	RELUCTANT	STABILITY

Maniac Magee Vocabulary

QUIVER	SLEAZY	COMMOTION	STUNNED	CRINGED
PRONE	EXPIRED	ECSTATIC	ENDURE	BLUNDERING
VAGUE	INCUBATING	FREE SPACE	COMPLIMENTS	WRENCHED
EXHAUSTION	MINUTELY	GAUNTLET	LURCHING	LUNGING
FORESIGHT	REPRISALS	PERILOUS	VENTURED	VACANT

Maniac Magee Vocabulary

APPARENTLY	SURGED	OPPONENT	DESOLATION	CONCLUSIONS
GRATES	CONFINED	CONVERGED	PANDEMONIUM	PROMPT
WRETCH	GRIZZLED	FREE SPACE	CLENCHED	HALTED
LUDICROUS	GROUSE	RANTING	DANGLED	INSTINCTS
BELLOWING	STABILITY	ROOKIE	LANGUISHED	INFAMOUS

Maniac Magee Vocabulary

GROUSE	CONFINED	PURSUERS	PERILOUS	CLENCHED
FATAL	EXUBERANCE	PREPOSTEROUS	APPARENTLY	FINICKY
EXHAUSTION	PRONE	FREE SPACE	EXPIRED	SCOFFING
SCOWLING	PROMPT	HALTED	FORESIGHT	CONTORTIONS
CONVERGED	QUIVER	SLEAZY	SOLITUDE	LANGUISHED

Maniac Magee Vocabulary

MAMMOTH	RICKETY	VAGUE	CRAMMED	ROOKIE
HOISTED	ESCORT	INSTINCTS	CUNNING	SURGED
REVEAL	GAUNTLET	FREE SPACE	SCANNED	LUDICROUS
CHAOTIC	STOIC	REPRISALS	SEETHING	DESOLATION
ENDURE	DUMBFOUNDED	MANIAC	RANDOM	PANDEMONIUM

Maniac Magee Vocabulary

APPARENTLY	EXPIRED	OPPONENT	CONTORTIONS	LANGUISHED
SEETHING	WRENCHED	INFAMOUS	CRINGED	ACCURATE
RICKETY	RANTING	FREE SPACE	FINICKY	MANIAC
GRATES	DESOLATION	ILLUSION	BELLOWING	DIGITS
SLEAZY	ECSTATIC	PRY	GROUSE	QUIVER

Maniac Magee Vocabulary

PRONE	INCUBATING	CONFINED	CONCLUSIONS	PREPOSTEROUS
GRIZZLED	INSTINCTS	FLINCHED	RANDOM	STABILITY
PURSUERS	SURGED	FREE SPACE	VACANT	SCANNED
STOIC	BLUNDERING	RELUCTANT	EXHAUSTION	COMMOTION
LUNGING	HOISTED	VAGUE	PROMPT	HALTED

Maniac Magee Vocabulary

DESOLATION	GRIZZLED	COMPLIMENTS	EXUBERANCE	PURSUERS
PREPOSTEROUS	MANIAC	STUNNED	OBVIOUS	PROMPT
GRATES	RELUCTANT	FREE SPACE	OPPONENT	LUDICROUS
COMMOTION	ENDURE	LUNGING	PERILOUS	LURCHING
SURGED	EXHAUSTION	PRONE	SCANNED	BELLOWING

Maniac Magee Vocabulary

MINUTELY	FINICKY	QUIVER	EXPIRED	CONFINED
STABILITY	VACANT	PRY	INSTINCTS	ROOKIE
DANGLED	LANGUISHED	FREE SPACE	APPARENTLY	CRAMMED
GAUNTLET	SCOFFING	SLEAZY	REPRISALS	MAMMOTH
SOLITUDE	STOIC	CONVERGED	VENTURED	ESCORT

Copyrighted

Maniac Magee Vocabulary

CUNNING	MANIAC	CONFINED	CONVERGED	CHAOTIC
LUDICROUS	SOLITUDE	PANDEMONIUM	CONCLUSIONS	INCUBATING
STABILITY	HOISTED	FREE SPACE	RICKETY	PRONE
CRINGED	FATAL	GRATES	EXUBERANCE	GAUNTLET
WRETCH	ACCURATE	PRY	CLENCHED	DESOLATION

Maniac Magee Vocabulary

SURGED	COMPLIMENTS	OBVIOUS	REVEAL	DIGITS
PROMPT	APPARENTLY	WRENCHED	OPPONENT	LURCHING
CONTORTIONS	SLEAZY	FREE SPACE	BELLOWING	SEETHING
GROUSE	PERILOUS	CRAMMED	INFAMOUS	RELUCTANT
DANGLED	ESCORT	MINUTELY	STOIC	COMMOTION

Maniac Magee Vocabulary

CONCLUSIONS	EXPIRED	FATAL	PROMPT	OPPONENT
SLEAZY	EXTORT	SEETHING	GRATES	HOISTED
ROOKIE	SURGED	FREE SPACE	CRAMMED	CONFINED
WRETCH	STUNNED	ECSTATIC	INSTINCTS	LUNGING
CLENCHED	WRENCHED	ESCORT	OBVIOUS	COMMOTION

Maniac Magee Vocabulary

PERILOUS	SOLITUDE	FINICKY	CUNNING	PRONE
FLINCHED	COMPLIMENTS	ILLUSION	EXHAUSTION	VENTURED
LUDICROUS	CHAOTIC	FREE SPACE	LURCHING	REVEAL
PRY	PREPOSTEROUS	INCUBATING	BLUNDERING	SCOFFING
PANDEMONIUM	SCANNED	STABILITY	DUMBFOUNDED	ACCURATE